MORMONISM UNMASKED

0-8054-1652-8

Published by Broadman & Holman Publishers, Nashville, Tennessee
Acquisitions & Development Editor: William D. Watkins
Typesetter: Leslie Joslin

Dewey Decimal Classification: 289.3
Subject Heading: MORMONISM
Library of Congress Card Catalog Number: 98-12749

Unless otherwise stated all Scripture citation is from the New King James *Version*, © 1979, 1980, 1982, Thomas Nelson, Inc., Publishers. Other versions include the NIV, Holy Bible, New International Version, © 1973, 1978, 1984 by International Bible Society.

Library of Congress Cataloging-in-Publication Data

Roberts, R. Philip.

Mormonism unmasked : confronting the contradictions between Mormonism beliefs and true Christianity / by R. Philip Roberts.

p. cm.

Includes bibliographical references.

ISBN 0-8054-1652-8

1. Mormon Church—Controversial literature. 2. Church of Jesus Christ of Latter-day Saints—Controversial literature.
I. Title.

BX8645.R63   1998   98-12749
289.3—dc21   CIP

1 2 3 4 5 02 01 00 99 98

MORMONISM UNMASKED

Confronting the Contradictions Between Mormon Beliefs and True Christianity

R. Philip Roberts

BROADMAN
& HOLMAN
PUBLISHERS
Nashville, Tennessee

For Anya—

Who can find a virtuous wife?
For her worth is far above rubies?
—PROVERBS 31:10

and for Dennis and Rauni—
who esteemed—

the reproach of Christ greater riches
than the treasures in Egypt.
—HEBREWS 11:26

CONTENTS

Acknowledgments   vii

Chapter 1: Mormons on Your Doorstep   1

Chapter 2: The Marketing of an Image   14

Chapter 3: The Making of a Religion   27

Chapter 4: Polytheism Reborn   45

Chapter 5: Confronting the Mormon Jesus   63

Chapter 6: This Is Good News?   76

Chapter 7: Revealing Revelations   95

Chapter 8: Jesus Is Coming Again   118

Chapter 9: By Whose Authority?   135

Chapter 10: Meeting the Mormon Challenge   152

Notes   172

Glossary   181

95247

V

ACKNOWLEDGMENTS

Like a dangerous journey fraught with difficulties and with many a twist and turn in the road, so is the production of a book on the topic of Mormon thought and theology. And just like a tough road, assistance is necessary along the way to reach your destination. Without the help of able and knowledgeable friends and associates, and two special cotravelers, this book would not have been possible.

First of all, a special thanks goes to Tal Davis, my associate director at the Interfaith Witness Division, and Sandra Tanner who helped complete the journey by the composition of several chapters in this book. Tal wrote the first chapter of the book, the fictional narrative about Dennis and Sue, and contributed chapters 5 and 7. Sandra wrote chapters 3, 4, and 9. Sandra and her husband, Jerald, have contributed more to evangelical understanding of Mormonism than any two persons—so Sandra's additions to this volume make it a particularly important book. Thank you, Sandra and Tal, for working so quickly under the time constraints under which this book was produced.

Bill Watkins of Broadman and Holman has been a delight to work with. He has made this book possible. Both Lisa Parnell and Becca Tyndall, neither of whom I've met except via the phone, lent to the adroit and unusually fast way in which this book was produced. Thank you, ladies, for your help. Joyce Johnson typed much of my material. In her usual way she did it well, quickly, and in her cheerful and Christlike manner.

Also, I want to thank Dennis and Rauni Higley who have become dear friends and encouragers and to whom part of the dedication has been ascribed. They have taught me much about Mormonism and always knew where the sources of information were and were always eager to answer my questions.

Lastly, I want to thank Anya, Mark, and Naomi, my family. Anya is doubtlessly worth "more than many [many] rubies." I could not find another one like her. Mark and Naomi are a joy to our lives because of their love for us and even more importantly because of their love for the Book and more critically the Lord of the Book, Jesus Christ. It is because of him and his eternal gospel that the Book was written. It is my prayer that the contents of this volume will honor him and will lead many to know the true Jesus.

—Phil Roberts

Chapter 1

MORMONS ON YOUR DOORSTEP

C all the toll-free number on your screen to order this free Bible. It is a gift from the Church of Jesus Christ of Latter-day Saints."

Joe hit the mute button on his remote control and quickly jotted down the number. "You know, I think I'd like to get one of those Bibles."

"We already have a couple of Bibles," his wife, Sue, said. "You don't read those very often. Why get another one?"

"Oh . . . I don't know," Joe mused, putting the pen behind his ear. "Maybe I just feel like it. If I had a new one, I might be motivated to study it more."

1

"Maybe we ought to start going to church," Sue said as she rubbed her bulging abdomen. "With the baby on the way, we really need to think about how we're going to raise him or her. Only two and a half more months to go."

"You're right!" Joe reached for the phone by his chair and dialed the number.

"Hello, may I help you?" a friendly woman's voice intoned.

"I'd like to order one of those free Bibles I saw offered on TV."

"Very fine, sir. If you give me your name, address, and phone number, one of our representatives will call you to deliver it."

"Oh!" Joe was surprised that the gift would be delivered, not mailed. "Well . . . OK. My name is Joe Murray." Then he gave her his address and phone number.

"Someone will call you in a few days to set up a time to bring the Bible. Thank you."

"Thank you," Joe replied and hung up the phone. He looked at Sue. "They're going to deliver our Bible in person. What church is it that's giving them away?"

"I think it's the Church of Latter-day Saints, or something like that."

"Yeah, that sounds right."

Two days later Joe and Sue were finishing dinner when the phone rang. "I'll get it," said Joe, picking up the receiver. "Hello."

"Mr. Murray?" asked a young male voice.

"Yes?"

"Mr. Murray, my name is Elder Watson. I'm a representative of the Church of Jesus Christ of Latter-day Saints here in your community. My associate and I would like to bring over the free Bible you ordered from the TV ads. Would tomorrow evening about this time be OK?"

"Sure," Joe said. "My wife and I'll be here."

"Great! Let me verify your address."

When the Murray's doorbell rang the next evening, Joe found two men in their late teens or early twenties at his front door. They were both wearing white dress shirts, dark slacks, and stylish ties. They both had name badges attached to the pockets of their shirts. Joe looked at the man closest to the door.

"Mr. Murray? I'm Elder Watson, and this is Elder Jones." Both men shook hands with Joe. "We're representatives from the Church of Jesus Christ of Latter-day Saints."

"Yes, come in," Joe said, gesturing toward the living room.

Sue walked from the kitchen to join them. "So you men represent your church?" she asked.

"That's right," Elder Watson replied. "We're both serving a two-year mission with the Church of Jesus Christ of Latter-day Saints. I'm from Utah, where I'll return in three months to finish college. Elder Jones is from California. He started his mission a few weeks ago."

Joe noticed Elder Watson was more relaxed. It was obvious he was more experienced.

"The Church of Jesus Christ of Latter-day Saints . . . isn't that the Mormon church?" Sue asked.

"It is?" Joe asked.

"Yes, ma'am," Elder Watson said. "But we prefer to be called the Church of Jesus Christ of Latter-day Saints. It's not Mormons' church; it's Christ's church."

"Mormons?" Joe blurted. "I thought you guys didn't believe in the Bible?"

Sue stared at him with a look that said, "Quiet! Be polite."

"Oh yes, sir, we believe and study the Bible as God's Word." Elder Watson reached into a knapsack filled with books and pulled out a beautifully bound King James Version of the Bible. "In fact, here's your free gift."

"Wow!" Joe beamed. "That's beautiful! Thank you." His eyes gleamed as he flipped through the crisp pages, as if to make sure it was the real thing. Then he looked at the young men. "I thought your church believed in some other book, the *Book of Mormon* or something."

"That's correct," smiled Elder Watson. "We do believe in the *Book of Mormon*." He reached in his knapsack and pulled out another book that looked like the Bible. "This is it. We believe it is a companion to the Bible. It doesn't replace the Bible or disagree with it, but it tells more about God and Jesus. Notice it's called *Another Testament of Jesus Christ.*"

3

"Another testament?" Sue asked.

"Yes," Elder Watson spoke confidently. "We believe that God has revealed to other prophets many other things besides what is in the Bible and has inspired men at other times. The *Book of Mormon* is a record of God's dealings with people on this continent and even how Jesus visited the Americas after his resurrection to proclaim the gospel here. We believe that it was translated miraculously by a modern prophet, Joseph Smith Jr., in the early 1800s."

"Yes," Elder Jones finally spoke up, "and we believe God is still revealing things to prophets today."

"So, are you really Christians?" Joe asked.

Sue glared at him.

"Absolutely!" replied Elder Watson. "We are definitely Christians. Remember what I said, it is the church of Jesus Christ. We have his name in the center of our church, and everything we do is centered around him."

"I see!" Joe was impressed. He had never met such confident and bright young men who were as excited as these men seemed to be about their religion. "My wife and I have been talking about going to church. We've been married about two years, and we're expecting our first child in a couple of months, as you can see."

The two young men looked at Sue and smiled. She blushed.

"Anyway, we're thinking about getting our family off on the right foot. Neither of us has been involved in church very much since we were kids. Oh, we attend now and then, and we do believe in God and Jesus, but we've just never found a church that appealed to us very much."

"I attended church regularly as a child," Sue said, "but when I was about fifteen, our church had a big split and our pastor was fired. My parents stopped going and so did I. It was very sad."

The two missionaries glanced at each other and said nothing.

Joe continued, "So Sue and I are interested in finding a church that can meet our family's needs and help us raise our children. When I saw the TV ad for the Bible, I felt I needed to start somewhere."

"Are you familiar at all with the teachings of the Church of Jesus Christ of Latter-day Saints?" Elder Watson asked.

"No, not really," Joe said. "I've heard that Mormons have good families. Is that true?"

"I would say that next to God and Jesus Christ, families are the most important things in our church." Elder Watson reached in his knapsack again and pulled out a VHS videotape. "This video is entitled *Families Are Forever.* Why don't we loan it to you? It will show how we believe families are important to people's spiritual lives." He handed it to Joe.

Joe took the video and asked, "Where is your church located, by the way?"

"The nearest ward meets about two miles from here," Elder Jones said. "Would you like to visit this Sunday? Our service begins at 10:30."

"Well, why not?" Joe said, smiling. He looked at Sue who nodded in agreement.

"Also, we have a series of home study lessons we would be happy to share with you," Elder Watson said. He handed Joe a small brochure. It had a picture of Jesus on the front and was entitled "The Plan of Our Heavenly Father."

"Would you like to study this with us? You can use your new Bible, and I'll loan you this *Book of Mormon.* Read it! I think you'll find it fascinating. In fact, there's a promise in the *Book of Mormon* that says if we read it prayerfully and ask the Heavenly Father if it's true, he will reveal it to us. Look at Moroni 10:4." Elder Watson handed the marked book to Joe.

Joe read the passage that was highlighted: "And when ye shall receive these things, I would exhort you that ye would ask God, the Eternal Father, in the name of Christ, if these things are not true; and if ye shall ask with a sincere heart, with real intent, having faith in Christ, he will manifest the truth of it unto you, by the power of the Holy Ghost."[1]

"I bear you my testimony that God has shown me that the *Book of Mormon* is true," Elder Jones said, "that Jesus is the Christ, that Joseph Smith is a prophet of God, and the Church of Jesus Christ of Latter-day Saints is his church."

"What do you mean 'bear your testimony'?" Sue asked.

"I mean that God has made it real to me." Elder Jones put his hand over his heart. "It's like a burning in my chest that has shown me this is true." He held up the *Book of Mormon.* "That's why I'm here on this mission, to tell others about it also."

Joe admired the men's strong convictions. He had never seen anyone so sure of his faith. "We'll visit your church this week. And, we'll do the studies with you. How about next week, same time?" He stood up and shook the hands of the two missionaries. "Thank you for coming. We'll see you Sunday."

"Just one more thing," Elder Watson said. "Could we have a prayer before we go?"

"Oh . . . sure," Joe said.

The four of them stood and bowed their heads as Elder Watson led: "Dear Heavenly Father, thank you for this time of sharing with Joe and Sue in their home. Dear Lord, we ask that you will help them understand the gospel of our Savior Jesus Christ. Help them see the truth of your church and find a strong foundation for their family. Thank you, in Jesus' name. Amen."

Joe and Sue were speechless. A tear trickled down Sue's cheek. No one had ever prayed for them before.

After the men left, Joe and Sue turned excitedly to look at their new Bible, the *Book of Mormon,* and the study brochure. "I think we may have found what we're looking for," Sue said.

"I still have some questions," Joe added. "But I've never seen such committed young people. We definitely should look into this some more. Let's watch this video."

Later that week Joe and Sue visited the local Latter-day Saints (LDS) ward worship service, also called the "sacrament meeting." Though the service seemed subdued, Joe and Sue were impressed by the warm welcome they received. They were also happy to see Elders Watson and Jones, who introduced them to the other worshipers.

"Where is your pastor?" Sue asked. "I'd like to meet him."

"Well, we don't exactly have a pastor like you may be thinking," Elder Watson said. "We have no paid ministers. All of our worthy men can have the priesthoods. We do have a bishop who is currently the leader of our ward."

Elder Watson introduced the couple to the ward's bishop, Mr. Johnson. He was a distinguished-looking man of about fifty who spoke gently and courteously. Joe and Sue learned he was a local lawyer.

"The missionaries told me you were going to visit today," Mr. Johnson said. "We sincerely hope you will investigate the beliefs of the Church of Jesus Christ of Latter-day Saints."

The Murrays were further impressed by the many young families they saw at the meeting. They noticed several couples about their age with children. It was obvious that families were a key ingredient in the church's value system.

Later that week the two missionaries returned to the home of Joe and Sue. The couple had read the brochure together, had looked up the listed Bible verses, and had begun reading the *Book of Mormon*. For the next six weeks the missionaries led the couple through a series of studies. The first, "The Plan of Our Heavenly Father," presented six beliefs to introduce them to Mormonism.

1. God the Father has a plan for our happiness. It is called the plan of salvation.
2. Jesus Christ has a central mission in the plan.
3. God reveals the truth about his plan through prophets.
4. The prophet Joseph Smith is a modern witness of Jesus Christ. Through him God has restored knowledge about the divine plan.
5. The *Book of Mormon* is another testament of Jesus Christ that clearly explains the divine plan.
6. Through the Holy Ghost each person can know that this message is true.[2]

The missionaries discussed these beliefs with the Murrays.

At the end of the lesson Joe spoke up. "I have no problem, of course, with the facts about God and Jesus, but I'm not sure about the rest, you know—Joseph Smith and all."

"Don't worry about it," Elder Watson said. "Just keep studying, read the *Book of Mormon* daily, and, above all, keep praying that God will show you that these things are true. Remember the promise of Moroni 10:4."

"OK, I'll keep praying. Like I said, I really liked what we learned about God and Jesus."

A week later, the second lesson focused more specifically on Jesus. It was titled "The Gospel of Jesus Christ." This lesson related seven basic principles.

1. Through the resurrection, we will be saved from physical death.

2. Through obedience to the principles and ordinances of the gospel of Jesus Christ, we can also be saved from sin.

3. In order to make the atonement effective in our lives, we must have faith in Christ.

4. We must repent of our sins.

5. We must be baptized by immersion to enter into a covenant with God.

6. We must receive the gift of the Holy Ghost to be spiritually reborn.

7. We must strive to obey all the commandments of God.[3]

Joe frowned. "I'm confused. I've been reading as you suggested. It's starting to make more sense now. Sue and I are really starting to feel led to join your church. You've mentioned baptism. I was baptized as an infant. Doesn't that count?"

"It must be performed by the proper authority and for the proper reason," Elder Watson said. "The authority must be the Aaronic Priesthood, and the purpose must be the remission or forgiveness of your sins. No other church has that authority. If you were baptized as an infant, how could you have repented of your sins?"

"I see what you mean," Joe said, nodding. "What's next?"

"Would you two like to be baptized by someone holding the priesthood authority?" Elder Watson asked. "We'll be having a baptismal service in a few weeks. Will you prepare yourselves for it?"

Joe and Sue looked at each other. "We'd like a little more time to think about it," Joe said.

"Fine," Elder Watson said. "We'll just keep going with our lessons until you decide you're ready. Just keep praying and ask the Spirit to tell you when. You'll feel it."

The third lesson, "The Restoration," dealt more with the founding and uniqueness of the Church of Jesus Christ of Latter-day Saints. The missionaries focused on six points.

1. Divine truth does not come from human sources. It comes from God, who revealed the truth through his apostles and prophets.
2. Because of the apostasy, the gift of revelation was lost for centuries.
3. God has again revealed the truth in our day through apostles and prophets of his restored church.
4. Through Joseph Smith, God restored the priesthood and reestablished the church of Jesus Christ.
5. We must come unto Christ by joining his church.
6. The members of the church receive great blessings by attending church meetings and partaking of the sacrament.[4]

"So, we come to Christ by joining his restored church?" Sue asked.

"That's correct," Elder Watson said. "That's what baptism is all about. Since the authority was lost when the true church was lost, no one could come to Christ, in the full sense of the word, until God restored the true church and the priesthood authority through Joseph Smith in 1830."

"I think I get it now," Joe said. "Sue and I have decided we want to get baptized. We're sure this is the church for us."

"The people are wonderful, and these teachings sure make sense. I don't remember getting such clear answers in the church where I grew up," Sue said. "When did you say the next baptism service will be?"

"In a few weeks," smiled Elder Watson. His heart was filled with pride and joy at their announcement. He had served nearly two years as an LDS missionary, and these were the first and probably only converts he would have the pleasure of baptizing. "Meanwhile, we'll finish up the rest of the lessons."

The fourth lesson was entitled "Eternal Progression" and focused on seven aspects of LDS doctrine regarding eternal life.

1. Before this mortal life, we lived with our Father in heaven.

2. The purpose of this mortal life is for us to prepare to become more like our Heavenly Father and return to him.

3. When we die, our spirits go to the spirit world.

4. The gospel is taught to the spirits in the spirit world, and the necessary ordinances are performed for them in temples.

5. The family can be an eternal unit.

6. The law of chastity teaches us how to govern the sacred power of procreation.

7. The word of wisdom is a divine law of health.[5]

"What exactly is the 'word of wisdom' again?" Joe asked.

"It's a commitment by church members to abstain from harmful substances," Elder Jones said, "especially alcohol, tobacco, coffee, tea, or harmful drugs."

"Well, we don't drink and smoke," said Sue, "and we certainly don't use drugs. But why the restriction on coffee and tea?"

"They contain caffeine," Elder Watson said, "which is known to be unhealthy."

"I suppose you're right," she said. "I guess I can do without my morning cup. I'll drink juice instead."

"And let me get this straight, we all lived before we were born?" Joe asked.

"Yes."

"And those who die without hearing the gospel can be saved?" Joe asked.

"Yes, by baptism for the dead in the temple."

"And we can be an eternal family?"

"Yes, you can be married for eternity if you are sealed together in a temple. It's all part of the Heavenly Father's plan."

"Boy, this is all new stuff to me. They never taught me any of this when I was a child in Sunday school," Sue said.

"There's so much more to come," Elder Watson said. "So much more to the gospel than you can ever know."

The fifth lesson was entitled "Living a Christ Like Life" and focused on four ethical and spiritual requirements of the LDS Church.

1. We should love God and our fellow men.
2. Sacrifice brings blessings.
3. Fasting and fast offerings bring us spiritual blessings.
4. The law of tithing helps us develop selflessness. [6]

"So one Sunday a month we're not supposed to eat but donate the money we'd spend for food to the church?" Sue asked.

"Yes, it's called a fast offering. The money will be used to care for the needy," answered Elder Watson.

"Makes sense to me," Sue concluded. "We eat too much anyway."

"Please explain the 'law of tithing' again," Joe asked.

"It simply means we give one-tenth of our income to the church for the Lord's work. If we do so, we will be blessed spiritually and temporally," Elder Watson said. "It's really a small price to pay when we consider all God has done for us."

"I suppose so," said Joe, as he mentally figured what his own tithing would amount to. "It won't be easy, but we can do it. After all, God expects it."

The final lesson before Joe and Sue were baptized was appropriately entitled "Membership in the Kingdom." Its six principles included the following points.

1. Jesus Christ is our Creator, Redeemer, Savior, and Judge.
2. Exaltation comes through Christ, and his church helps us progress toward perfection.
3. The church and its members have a responsibility for perfecting the saints.
4. The church and its members have a responsibility for proclaiming the gospel.

5. The church and its members have a responsibility for redeeming the dead.

6. We can follow the straight and narrow path to perfection.[7]

"So, in a sense, we are all missionaries," Joe said. "I'm unclear on one thing though. Exaltation means we can progress to become like our Heavenly Father?"

"Yes," nodded the missionaries.

"But that's different from the atonement of Christ, right?"

"Correct," explained Elder Watson. "Exaltation is what happens after Christ's atonement. He died so all could be raised from the dead. However, exaltation is for those who strive for perfection and keep the commandments and ordinances of the gospel, starting with baptism."

"Great, let's do it!" said Joe.

The next Sunday Joe and Sue were baptized by Elder Watson. Joe and Sue thanked him for all he had done for them and embarked on what they saw as a new life as members of the Church of Jesus Christ of Latter-day Saints. They were now full-fledged Mormons and were determined to live up to everything the religion expected of them.

The above story is fictional, but it is not fictitious. Last year more than three hundred thousand people worldwide made the same commitments Joe and Sue did and were baptized as converts into the LDS Church. Many of those were just like the Murrays—people looking for answers and a foundation for their lives and families. The Church of Jesus Christ of Latter-day Saints has one of the most effective and efficient missionary programs of any religious group in the world today, with more than fifty-five thousand full time missionaries serving in more than 160 countries. Also, LDS membership has doubled since 1981, and now has a membership of more than ten million worldwide with about half of their members in North America.

Thus, the LDS presents a major challenge to Christian churches, especially since many LDS converts are taken from among Christian church memberships. This brings us to the crux of the matter and to the primary purposes for this book. We intend to answer the following six crucial questions regarding the LDS Church and its doctrines.

1. What is the scope of the LDS Church, and why is it growing at such a phenomenal rate worldwide?

2. How did the LDS Church begin, and why has controversy followed it throughout its history?

3. What does the LDS Church teach, and, perhaps most important of all, is Mormonism an authentic Christian system?

4. Are Mormon teachings compatible with biblical doctrines?

5. What should be the appropriate response to Mormons and the LDS Church?

6. Should Christians seek to evangelize Mormons, and if so, what is the most effective way?

These and other questions will be addressed in the chapters to follow. All non-Mormons, especially orthodox Christians, should be fully aware of the facts about Mormonism. Otherwise, like Joe and Sue, they may be unable to respond adequately when Mormons come knocking on their doors.

Chapter 2

THE MARKETING OF AN IMAGE

W hat our fictitious couple, Joe and Sue Murray, experienced in chapter 1 is certainly not make-believe. Currently, the more than fifty thousand Mormon missionaries worldwide spend most of their time as the two energetic quasi-evangelists did with Joe and Sue— seeking to convince people of the claims of Joseph Smith and the truths of Mormon scripture.

Additionally, the Mormon Church has mounted an aggressive public relations campaign. Using attractive, inviting television commercials with an offer for a free *Book of Mormon* or a Bible, Mormonism portrays itself nationwide as a mainstream Christian movement. This large and expensive public relations drive is fueled by the LDS Church's investments in American economic life, as well as by the giving of its own members.

In this chapter we'll look at the proselytizing strategy of this organization, its public relations profile, and its financial resources.

PUBLIC RELATIONS AND CONVERTS

The mainstay of Mormon growth is its missionary corps. Young men and women in their late teens or early twenties spend up to two years sharing the gospel of Mormonism. Fifteen missionary training centers dot the globe. The largest is in Provo, Utah, which is fed by the almost thirty thousand undergraduates at nearby Mormon-operated Brigham Young University.

Many Mormon missionaries were raised in LDS families and were exposed to the teaching of Mormonism from infancy. Children's books based on the *Book of Mormon* or even the *Articles of Faith* of the church often were their reading staples. The budding missionaries attended Mormon Sunday school, were baptized at age eight (as the church directs for Mormon children), and usually attended early morning "seminary" classes during their high school careers.

At the college level, a manual entitled *Doctrines of the Gospel* is used to further ground Mormons in their faith. From it they learn about the great "apostasy" of Christianity, the appearances of God, Jesus, and other biblical figures to Joseph Smith. They also learn about the distinctive views of Mormonism regarding God, Jesus, and the "gospel."

Their parents usually are diligent about saving and encouraging their children's saving for their eventual Mormon mission. All costs for proselytizing ventures are paid by the youth or their parents alone. The church pays for their return trip home at the end of the two-year mission.

When young persons begin their missionary service, they are trained at a missionary training center. At the centers, the young missionaries learn to cook, wash, iron, and do other household chores. If their missionary destination is a non-English-speaking country, they learn some of its language. But most important, they learn how to present the claims of Mormonism in the most positive and attractive way possible.

Once committed to a Mormon mission, missionaries have no contact with their families except for letters and two phone calls a year, which can be made on Christmas and Mother's Day. A Mormon missionary's time and energy is to be spent zealously seeking converts to the LDS Church.

The Bottom Line of Missions

Converting others to the church is the bottom line of the Mormon missionary. Mormonism is built on the concept that a person must be baptized by a priesthood "holder" or an active male member of the church to achieve the highest level of salvation. That level is the celestial kingdom. Mormonism therefore practices proselytization, or the conversion of a person, not just to faith in the Christ of Mormonism but to the Mormon Church itself. While evangelical Christians and other Bible-based Christian missionaries may have a limited goal of leading people to faith in Jesus Christ, Mormonism's real intent is baptism and active membership in their church. It is the Mormon's conviction that the one true Church is the Church of Jesus Christ of Latter-day Saints.

Mormons therefore proselytize members of Christian churches, encouraging them to leave and renounce the validity of their own denominations. Converts are to be baptized by a member of the priesthood in the LDS Church to become Mormons. Mormons believe baptism by immersion and other acts are absolutely essential for converts to become active participants in the LDS Church so they may become faithful and genuine followers of Jesus in this life.

Bible-based Christians believe that faith in Jesus alone saves. While true believers are members of Christ's universal Body, the Church, they do not have to join a particular denomination to be fully obedient followers of Christ. Therefore evangelism, the sharing of the truth of Christ—his saving death and victorious resurrection—and not proselytization, marks Christian missionary efforts.

How successful are Mormon missionaries? On average, each Mormon missionary leads approximately six people each year into the ranks of the Mormon Church. The church's goal is to improve its proselytizing methods and thereby raise the average number of converts. The church also is working to increase its number of missionaries. By 2005 to 2010, the Mormon hierarchy hopes to have one hundred thousand Mormon missionaries active around the world. Their strategy and logic are simple: the more people contacted, the more likely that the number of converts will increase. If the average number of converts per missionary remains the same or increases, the likelihood is that Mormonism will have a half-million to a million converts a year by 2010.

The Tactics of Appeal

How is it that Christians develop an interest in the "fulness of the gospel" as offered by the LDS Church? First, Mormons appeal to people's interests in knowing more about Jesus Christ. Wouldn't every sincere Christian like to know more about the life and ministry of Jesus? Of course! And the Mormons have it, they claim, in the *Book of Mormon: Another Testament of Jesus Christ*. The *Book of Mormon*, they assert, fills in many of the important gaps in Christ's life—like his visit to the Western Hemisphere to the tribes of the Nephites and Lamanites. Even though these claims are fallacious and contradict all that historians and anthropologists know about the Americas, Mormon apologists strive to present a strong case for their interpretation of the "facts." Christians can often be hooked if they are not well acquainted with the Bible and with the unreliability and contrived nature of the *Book of Mormon*.

A second approach often used by the missionaries is to appeal to people's love for families. Mormons have expended enormous effort in building a reputation for family values. Mormons frequently have large, attractive, middle-class families. Mormon missionaries encourage interest and involvement in their church to strengthen family ties and values. But the appeal of Mormonism goes beyond the here and now and extends to eternity. Mormonism says that if you are married in their temples, your children are sealed to you. If the whole family obeys and serves the church, then they will spend eternity together.

This futuristic scenario sounds very attractive to many people. However, it has no support in the Bible or in centuries of Christian teaching. In fact, it is Jesus who told us that those who are resurrected to a new life in heaven "neither marry nor are given in marriage, but are like angels of God in heaven" (Matt. 22:30). Death severs the marital bond between husband and wife, and resurrection does not restore it. In heaven, Christ's church is married to him; the divine Groom is forever bonded to his bride, the Christian church, which constitutes all people who have trusted in him by faith (Rev. 21:9–27). In him believing families are united eternally, not through the Mormon promise of celestial exhaltation and godhood.

Mormonism also appeals to people by offering the possibility of helping deceased relatives and friends. Much of the system of temple rituals and sacred or secret ceremonies is designed to promote deceased non-Mormons from spirit prison to the far more favorable position of paradise. This elevation of spirits can only be accomplished by proxy baptism and marriage in a Mormon temple. Mormonism claims that not only the recently dead, but ancestors as far back as they can be traced are able to be liberated from spirit prison. The extensive genealogical studies of the LDS Church are based on their teachings that the dead can be evangelized. It is no surprise, then, that the largest and most extensive genealogical records in the world are in the possession of the Mormon Church. Often the use of these materials is offered, free of charge, to non-Mormons. Interest in one's heritage (for Mormons and non-Mormons) is encouraged, since once a person is exposed to the resources that Mormonism offers, he can then be cultivated as a prospect for LDS membership.

People with recently deceased family members or friends are often drawn to this hope for salvation after death. But here again, Mormonism runs up against biblical teaching that tells us that "it is appointed for men to die once, but after this the judgment"

(Heb. 9:27). Decision time for the afterlife is in the present. There are no second chances for salvation after death—only judgment.

Another attraction to the Church of Jesus Christ of Latter-day Saints is that it is the "one true Church." After all, who would want to be a part of a false church or incomplete fellowship of congregations? LDS doctrine claims that the Mormon prophet, president of the church, and sole revelator of God is able to give guidance and reveal God's will to his people, Latter-day Saints. Young people and families often are equally attracted to the possibilities of "extra" assistance in determining the best answers to life's choices. It is the claim of Mormonism that only the LDS Church and its prophet can provide the safety of God's leadership.

The advocation and promotion of traditional Christian morality, albeit in Mormon dress, is another point of attraction for non-Mormons. In a confusing world where some Christian churches tolerate promiscuous and adulterous relationships and even homosexuality, Mormonism is an obviously conservative alternative. Missionaries themselves project this image. Their clean-cut personas with short hair, white shirts, and ties are apparent to all.

Non-Mormons may choose to join the LDS Church not so much because of doctrine, but because of the church's carefully crafted image as an upholder of morality and traditional values. Once a part of the organization, the succeeding generations of Mormons from the families of converts learn the fine points of Mormon theology. These doctrinal issues include exaltation to godhood, the rites and rituals of the temple essential to perform for admission into the celestial kingdom, as well as the unique position of the church regarding Jesus and proxy baptism for the dead.

Once individuals or couples are visited by missionaries and show an interest in the claims of Mormonism, the next step is for them to view proselyting videos. There are various titles and types of tapes. Included among them are such titles as *The Heavenly Father's Plan* and *On the Way Home.*

Generally the claim of the LDS Church to be the one true Church, the fact that LDS baptism is essential for eternal progression, and questions raised about the integrity of the Bible are not mentioned by the missionaries to potential converts. Instead, cautious and encouraging comments are made about God being our Heavenly Father, Jesus being our big brother, and families staying together forever. By emphasizing these positive elements, Mormon missionaries effectively lessen the possibility of rejection by potential converts.

Following a video, there are usually six lessons led by a missionary. The basic Mormon concepts previously mentioned are repeated in further detail. *Gospel Principles* is the last introduction to Mormonism made to prospective converts prior to their induction into the church via baptism. This manual cites pieces of Mormon literature, which are carefully interwoven with Bible verses.

The LDS Church takes incremental and carefully planned steps in its attempt to proselytize people away from Christianity into Mormonism. Unfortunately, the LDS Church's efforts are often very effective.

PUBLIC RELATIONS AND FINANCIAL RESOURCES

The Church of Jesus Christ of Latter-day Saints is not only an aggressive proselytizing church, but it is also a powerful economic machine. The entire missionary and public relations effort of the LDS Church is supported by its massive economic resources. These finances are generated, first of all, by the tithes of individual Mormons and their families.

Tithing, or the donation of one-tenth of personal financial income to church causes, is part of the teaching and biblical understanding of many Christian churches. Many evangelical Christians and their denominations encourage its practice. Mormonism, however, adds a nonbiblical dimension to this otherwise Bible-based virtue, teaching that tithing is essential to gain the celestial kingdom. Tithing, therefore, becomes a work that contributes toward achieving a higher level of salvation. Approximately one-third of Mormonism's five million U.S. members are temple-worthy and therefore tithers. *Time* magazine estimated that in 1996, $5.2 billion in tithes flowed into the Mormon church headquarters in Salt Lake City, with $4.9 billion coming from American church members.[1] Church authorities in Salt Lake City direct the funds, helping to construct more than three hundred chapels or ward houses each year and several new temples. The missionary support enterprise itself receives approximately $500 million dollars each year.

The LDS Church is also a large investment empire. Since the general authorities of Mormonism are comprised of business executives, there is a built-in stratum of money-making minds within the church hierarchy. While most Christian churches and denominations use investments to support retirement programs for their pastors and workers, with other funds going directly to support ongoing ministries, Mormons use high-powered investments to produce an empire of financial enterprise.

How big is the Mormon financial kingdom? Recent estimates calculate that it produces $5.9 billion a year and contains more than $30 billion in assets. Apart from Mormon temples and meeting houses, the Mormon empire owns sixteen radio stations, one television station, a daily Salt Lake City newspaper *(Deseret News)*, a book company, and a large agricultural enterprise with one ranch outside of Orlando, Florida, alone worth $858 million. It also owns and operates Utah's largest department store chain (ZCMI). All of these enterprises are operated by Deseret Management Corporation, the business arm of the LDS Church. These commercial enterprises make Mormonism the largest religious financial enterprise in the United States, outside of the Roman Catholic Church.

Is Mormonism gaining converts? Are they successful in their proselytizing efforts? Numbers alone tell us yes. Growth in the U.S. is approximately 5 percent a year, while overseas it increases at approximately 10 percent. In 1950 there were only 1 million Latter-day Saints worldwide. Adherents now total approximately 10.6 million, with forecasts of the number of Mormons worldwide exceeding 250 million within the next century. The Church of Jesus Christ of Latter-day Saints has become a worldwide movement with a small majority of its members now living outside the U.S.[2]

The mere number of members does not tell the whole story. Only one-fourth to one-third of Mormons, at most, are actually temple-worthy and therefore tithing contributors to LDS work. There is a severe shortage of Mormon male leaders in Latin America, as well as the Philippines, while most of funding for international mission work still comes principally from the intermontane western region of the United States. Top leadership in the church is dominated by the American pioneer stock who can trace their lineage back to the trek west under Brigham Young's leadership.

When and how will the church find a place for internationals in the management and direction of the church? Will Mormons continue to adequately fund overseas growth, including temple construction, from a U.S. base of support? Will strict conformity to American-produced literature continue to appeal to internationals?[3] All of these are practical questions without solutions. The main question, however, is will the world's approximately one billion professing Christians buy the Mormons' argument that they are not only a new and improved form of Christianity but the only true expression of the Church on earth?

PUBLIC RELATIONS
AND POPULAR OPINION

The traditional and aggressive missionary program of the LDS Church is complemented by a sophisticated public relations element. The public image of the church is fine-tuned to present the image of Mormonism as the best and most complete form of Christianity. One Mormon thinker has expressed it as Mormonism being a one-hundred-watt light bulb in the wattage of Christianity while other churches are forty or sixty watts.[4] This type of posturing attempts to soften the hard line drawn by Joseph Smith when he founded the church. That hard line was the declaration that all Christian denominations were wrong, their confessions an abomination, and their professors and members corrupt.[5]

While Mormonism tries to soften its critique of Christians, it more emphatically seeks acceptance as a Christian religion. In 1982 additional words were added to the *Book of Mormon* to give it the subtitle *Another Testament of Jesus Christ*. The official logo of the church was altered as well in the early 1990s by making the name

"Jesus Christ" three times larger than the words "The Church of" and "Latter-day Saints."

Visitors to Temple Square in Salt Lake City over the last twenty years have noted a dramatic shift in visitor displays. The emphasis has been taken off Joseph Smith and the foundation of the Mormon Church. Instead, the prominent murals displayed in the visitors center are biblical paintings featuring the person and work of Jesus Christ. Visitors are informed that the church emphasizes the person of Jesus Christ and that Latter-day Saints are folk who have a true and living relationship with Christ. If visitors are interested in pure, undiluted Mormonism, they must cross the street to the church's history museum or visit the remote displays in the southeast corner of the square. At the same time church officials declare that "We are Christians!" *USA Today* promoted the headline "Christian but different," adding "Members of the Church of Jesus Christ of Latter-day Saints say they are Christian but neither Protestant nor Catholic."[6]

Perhaps no one has achieved more positive good for the LDS "Christian" makeover than author and motivator Stephen Covey. Covey is renowned as the author of the long-term best-seller *The Seven Habits of Highly Effective People.* He is heralded as a pioneer in the advocacy of spiritual values for the makers and shakers and wannabes of American society. Among other issues, he encourages the reading of "scripture," prayer, and other spiritual disciplines. A closer look at his religious and theological presuppositions, however, demonstrates that much of what Covey is attempting to do is condition people toward Mormonism. In fact, he has declared himself a virulent enemy of Christian truth.

Prior to writing *Seven Habits,* Covey penned *The Divine Center,*[7] aimed strictly at Mormons and a precursor to his best-seller. There he states that any spiritual guide other than Mormonism is a false "map" that will limit a person's spiritual development. Additionally he maintains that Joseph Smith was correct to identify the "creeds of the [Christian] fathers" as "the very mainspring of all corruption."[8] He warns readers against seeking "any kind of 'special relationship'" with Jesus Christ.[9] Covey maintains that salvation by grace alone—the mainstay of salvation, according to the Bible—is a "false concept" and an "apostate doctrine."[10] In place of these essential truths, he says that Mormon truths can equip people with "godlike powers and capacities."[11]

For Covey the bottom line is to influence people, even indirectly, toward the teachings of the LDS Church: "I have found in speaking to various non-LDS groups in different cultures that we can teach and testify of many gospel principles [i.e., Mormonism] if we are careful in selecting words which carry our meaning but come from their experience and frame of mind."[12] Whether or not he is immediately successful in proselytizing non-Mormons does not seem to be of first importance to Covey. He is, nevertheless, anxious to condition them to be more positive about Mormonism.

Darl Anderson is the author of *Soft Answers to Hard Questions: Building Bridges for Better Understanding*. While Anderson is less well known than Covey, his target audience for his Mormon apologetics program is Protestant ministers. His approach is to offer polite and appealing responses to the tough questions that are often placed to Mormons regarding the secret temple ceremonies, racist attitudes of the Mormon god, and Mormons becoming gods. Anderson knows that Christian ministers are "the main source of public opinion about religion" and that they exercise "a tremendous impact on what people think about the LDS faith."[13]

While on the surface it might appear that all Anderson desires is to build better ecumenical ties between LDS and Protestants, a closer look demonstrates that he believes Mormonism is the only true belief system and that the LDS "Church is divine and [has the] most effective plan to gain these gifts of heaven."[14] His agenda is to promote Mormonism as the way to God's blessings and the "fulness" of salvation.

There are other public relations emphases within Mormonism, including a recent attempt to discourage the use of the term "Mormon." Mormon was allegedly the compiler and preserver of the *Book of Mormon* who delivered the "golden plates" to his son Moroni just prior to the last battle at Cumorah, which destroyed the righteous Nephites in A.D. 400. Moroni later revealed to Joseph Smith, it is believed, the location of the plates (which were the "source" of the *Book of Mormon*). The name Mormon has stuck to the LDS Church almost from its inception. Due to the negative connotation of the word *Mormon* and its identification with anti-Christian beliefs, now the "Mormons urge use of formal name"— The Church of Jesus Christ of Latter-day Saints.[15]

Is the attempt to redesign the Mormon image working? Well, at least one evangelical poll, the Barna Report, now shows that up to 26 percent of all Mormons are genuinely born again. (The Mormon doctrine of baptism and the subsequent laying on of hands for the reception of the Holy Ghost are now understood and interpreted by Mormons as the new birth.) Even former President Jimmy Carter has declared that Mormons are Christian in spite of their nonbiblical views of God, Jesus, and salvation.[16]

On the surface, Mormons sometimes look and sound Christian. Mormon leaders have created a public relations campaign to promote the LDS Church as Christian, and they have a financial empire to support their efforts. For people who are uninformed about what Mormonism really teaches and what Mormons truly believe, the LDS campaign will continue to make a positive impression.

The Bible calls on followers of the true Jesus Christ to judge righteously (John 7:24). We are to draw conclusions that are accurate and based on facts. That's what we plan to do in these pages as we unmask Mormonism.

WITNESSING POINTS

- The LDS Church's goal is to represent itself as Christian while maintaining Mormon doctrines and distinctions.
- The *Book of Mormon* is now subtitled *Another Testament of Jesus Christ* to appeal to people "who love Jesus."
- Mormons appeal to those who are concerned about the souls of deceased friends and relatives, promoting baptism for the dead. But the Bible does not teach or advocate baptism for the dead.
- Mormon missionaries view their good works as a step toward the celestial kingdom. So emphasize to them that God's grace in Christ is sufficient for salvation.
- Remember that the Bible is the ultimate source for family guidance, not any other book, church, or organization. Also, families who are Bible-based generally have healthy and happy homes.
- Mormonism is not just a cult in terms of doctrine; it is a culture that seeks to attract and hold people and their families for generations.

Chapter 3

THE MAKING OF A RELIGION

*I have more to boast of than ever any man had. I am the
only man that has ever been able to keep a whole church
together since the days of Adam. A large majority of the
whole have stood by me. Neither Paul, John, Peter, nor
Jesus ever did it. I boast that no man ever did such a work
as I. The followers of Jesus ran away from Him; but the
Latter-day Saints never ran away from me yet.*

—JOSEPH SMITH, *History of the Church*

J oseph Smith, born December 23, 1805, in Sharon,
Vermont, was the fourth child of a struggling farmer
and occasional schoolteacher. Although the father
Smith was a religious man, he claimed no church
membership. After falling on hard times, the family made
several moves, finally settling on a farm in the booming
area of Manchester, just south of Palmyra, New York, in
1816. (Later, this part of New York would be known as the
"burnt over" district following the revivals of the Second
Great Awakening.) Here the Smiths and their eight children tried to climb out from under their growing debts.

Besides farming, the family occasionally supplemented their meager earnings by selling such items as gingerbread and root beer. During this time, Joseph and his father became increasingly engaged in folk magic, using magical seer stones and divining rods to look for buried treasure and lost items.[1]

JOSEPH SMITH'S FIRST VISION

Due to a tremendous revival in his neighborhood in 1820, Joseph Smith became concerned about which church he should join, noting in his later writings that "Some were contending for the Methodist faith, some for the Presbyterian, and some for the Baptist." Joseph's mother, sister, and brother had joined the Presbyterian church.

Faced with this dilemma, Smith decided only God could tell him which church was right.

> So, in accordance with this, my determination to ask of God, I retired to the woods to make the attempt. . . . When the light rested upon me, I saw two personages, whose brightness and glory defy all description, standing above me in the air. One of them spake unto me, calling me by name and said, pointing to the other—*This is My Beloved Son. Hear Him!*
>
> My object in going to inquire of the Lord was to know which of all the sects was right, that I might know which to join. . . . I asked the Personages who stood above me in the light, which of all the sects was right (for at this time it had never entered into my heart that all were wrong)—and which I should join. I was answered that I must join none of them, for they were all wrong; and the Personage who addressed me said that all their creeds were an abomination in his sight; that those professors were all corrupt; that: "they draw near to me with their lips, but their hearts are far from me, they teach for doctrines the commandments of men."[2]

On the basis of this vision, Mormons declare that God has rejected all other churches, and that no one outside the Church of Jesus Christ of Latter-day Saints has the authority to baptize or act for God. They also point to this vision as proof that God the Father and Jesus Christ both have physical, resurrected bodies and are totally separate gods.

SMITH'S SECOND VISION

Smith also claimed that in 1823 an angel appeared to him, announcing that Smith was chosen of God to translate an ancient record hid in a nearby hill. Moroni, the being who appeared to Joseph Smith, was the last man to record the events of his civilization. Moroni then buried the record, knowing it must be hidden away until the last days. Smith was told to meet with Moroni each September 22 until God felt it was the right time to allow Smith to obtain the record. This record was inscribed on gold plates in reformed Egyptian, and it told of God's dealings with the former inhabitants of the land, including a visit from Jesus Christ to America after his crucifixion. These plates allegedly contained the history of a prophet named Lehi and his family, who migrated from Jerusalem about 600 B.C. and brought civilization to the American continents. The angel informed Smith that the record contained "the fulness of the everlasting Gospel . . . as delivered by the Savior to the ancient inhabitants; also, that there were two stones in silver bows [somewhat like spectacles] . . . called the Urim and Thummim . . . and that God had prepared them for the purpose of translating the book."[3]

Finally, in 1827, Smith was allowed to take the records and the Urim and Thummim from their hiding place in the hill and began the translation. The stones were to provide the translation, with Smith merely reading the text to his scribe. The scribe's recordings were then published in 1830 and entitled the *Book of Mormon*.

HISTORY OR FANTASY?

There are numerous problems with Smith's account of his early life.

He did not publish his account of his first vision until 1842, twenty-two years after the alleged event. At this time he was more than a thousand miles from the area at which he supposedly had his vision, thus lessening the chance of having someone from the New York area challenge his account.

The revival that Smith described as supposedly stirring his mind to seek out the true church did not happen until 1824–25, not in the year 1820 as he claimed. This discrepancy throws off his whole chronology. Protestant church records show that revivals occurred in the area before 1820 and again in 1824–25, but not during the year he specifies. For his story to be consistent, his first vision would have had to occur before the angel came to him in 1823.

Another problem with Smith's 1842 printed account is the implication that, as of 1820, Joseph Smith was teaching that the Father and the Son both had physical bodies, thus making them totally separate gods. The early documents of Mormonism show that during the 1820s and early 1830s, Smith was teaching there was only one God. His plural god doctrine was not put forward until the 1840s in Nauvoo, Illinois.[4]

Over the last thirty-five years, many of Smith's early papers have been published. We now have other early accounts of Smith's first vision that relate the story differently. In a handwritten account that Smith wrote in 1831–32, he said he was fifteen when "the Lord" appeared to him. Not only is his age different, but he described only one being, as opposed to the "two personages" he had previously accounted for, in the vision. Then in 1835, Smith told his story to a visitor and stated that he was fourteen when he had his first vision in which he saw "many angels." Also in the account of 1831–32, Smith mentioned that he had already concluded that all churches were in apostasy before he went into the woods to pray, while the official account of 1842 states that he had not concluded this until God so informed him in the vision. Thus we have different accounts of the number of beings who appeared in Smith's first vision, who they were, and what they said.

The earliest LDS publication to print a "full history" of the rise of Mormonism, the *Messenger and Advocate*, failed to mention Smith's vision in 1820, starting instead with the angel appearing in Smith's bedroom in 1823.[5]

Other discrepancies in Joseph Smith's story emerge when his official account of his early years is compared with documents and statements of those around him at the time. Supposedly from age fourteen to twenty-one (1820–27), Smith was being prepared by the Lord for the great restoration work ahead of him. Yet during this time he was engaged in folk magic and was occasionally hired to use his magical stone—found in a neighbor's (Mr. Chase) well—to find buried treasures and lost objects. Since the Lord had so specifically instructed the nation of Israel not to engage in any magical practices,[6] it is hard to believe that God would choose a magician to restore his church.

In 1826 Smith's failure to find any treasure for Josiah Stowell led to his arrest on the charge of being a disorderly person, a "glass looker" (crystal ball user). On March 20, 1826, he was brought before Albert Neely, justice of the peace, in Bainbridge, New York. The court record states that Smith had used a stone placed in his hat to find treasures or lost property "for three years" prior to 1826.[7] While he was searching for buried treasures in the employment of Mr. Stowell, he was boarding with the Isaac Hale family. Mr. Hale objected to Smith's method of searching for treasures, and he opposed Smith's courtship of Hale's beautiful, twenty-one-year-old daughter, Emma. Parental disapproval was no obstacle to Smith: when Mr. and Mrs. Hale were away on a trip in January of 1827, Joseph and Emma eloped.[8]

Reports of witnesses also differ from Smith's own account of the translation process. Did he use the Urim and Thummim, prepared by God and stored with the plates, to translate the record, or did he use the chocolate-colored stone found in Mr. Chase's well? In 1870 Martin Harris, one of the three witnesses to the *Book of Mormon*, described in a public speech the *Book of Mormon* translation process. This address, published in a Mormon document, *Historical Record*, stated, "[T]he Prophet possessed a seer stone, by which he was enabled to translate as well as from the Urim and Thummim, and for convenience he then used the seer stone."[9] David Whitmer, one of the three witnesses allegedly shown the plates by an angel, said this: "I will now give you a description of the manner in which the *Book of Mormon* was translated. Joseph would put the seer stone into a hat, and put his face in the hat, drawing it closely around his face to exclude the light; and in the darkness the spiritual light would shine. A piece of something resembling parchment would appear, and on that appeared the writing."[10] This is the same magic stone and method that he used to search for buried treasures.

Another puzzling event was Joseph Smith's attempt to join the Methodist Church in 1828, eight years after the Father and Son allegedly told him that all the churches were apostate, therefore none worthy of joining. Why did he ignore God's command to "join none of them"?[11]

RESTORATION OF THE
TRUE CHURCH OF CHRIST

The LDS Church teaches that when Christ first set up his church, it contained both the Aaronic and Melchizedek priesthoods, which provided the authority necessary for one to act in the name of God and to perform such rites as baptism.

Mormons claim that the early Christian church contained all the same teachings the LDS embrace today. However, with the death of Christ's apostles, they believe the church fell into total apostasy, instituted false doctrine, changed the Scriptures, and lost the authority to minister in God's name. Mormonism claims that every baptism performed by a minister outside of the true Church of Christ is rejected by God.[12] Not until Joseph Smith restored the "only true church" with the priesthood authority was a person able to have a valid baptism.

Joseph Smith claimed that on May 15, 1829, John the Baptist appeared to him and Oliver Cowdery and bestowed on them the keys of the Aaronic priesthood, thus giving them the authority to perform valid baptisms.[13] Smith claimed that a month later the apostles Peter, James, and John appeared to him and Cowdery and bestowed on them the Melchizedek priesthood. This priesthood, lost since the time of the original apostles, is supposed to be necessary to ordain any man as a minister of God. With these two priesthoods restored, Smith had the correct authority to reestablish the "only true church."

The LDS concept of a total apostasy contradicts Christ's promise that "I will build My church, and the gates of Hades shall not prevail against it" (Matt. 16:18). Also, the Book of Hebrews explains that the Aaronic priesthood was brought to an end with the death of Christ and that Christ is our only eternal High Priest "after the order of Melchizedek." (See Heb. 3:1; 4:14–16; 5:1–9; 6:20; 7:11–28.)

Joseph Smith set up his new church on April 6, 1830, in New York, with himself as the "first elder" and five other members. Two months later the *Book of Mormon* was published, financed by *Book of Mormon* witness Martin Harris.

Smith's fledgling church adopted many of the same teachings of Thomas and Alexander Campbell, early advocates of the need for a restoration of New Testament Christianity. These men rejected church creeds, taught baptismal regeneration, rejected infant baptism, and had communion every week.

Originally, Joseph Smith named his church "The Church of Christ," but in 1834, he changed it to "The Church of the Latter Day Saints." Then in 1838 Smith received a revelation to change the name once again to "The Church of Jesus Christ of Latter-day Saints."[14]

THE OHIO-MISSOURI YEARS

As soon as Smith's new church was organized, it began sending out missionaries. The *Book of Mormon* teaches that the Lamanites (Native Americans) are Israelites and must have the gospel taken to them before Christ returns. In the latter part of 1830, several men were sent to preach to the Indians in Ohio and Missouri.

Their real success came when they encountered an unconventional Baptist minister by the name of Sidney Rigdon. Rigdon had worked with the Campbells and taught his congregation many of the same doctrines. After hearing the missionaries tell of the *Book of Mormon* and the great work of restoring the New Testament church in preparation for the coming of Christ, Rigdon traveled to New York to meet Joseph Smith. After Rigdon accepted Mormonism,

Joseph immediately put him to work as his scribe on his new translation of the Bible. Although the work of translating the Bible is commanded in Smith's revelations, the Mormons have never printed the entire work.[15] There are portions of Smith's corrections printed at the back of LDS Bibles, but not the whole text.

During the winter Joseph Smith traveled back to Ohio with Rigdon. They were able to convince many families from Rigdon's former church to join the Mormons.[16] In January of 1831, Smith received a revelation that the New York Mormons should "assemble together at the Ohio."[17] Over 150 people from the three New York branches of Smith's church migrated to the Kirtland, Ohio, area. Other Mormons were sent to build up a colony in Independence, Missouri. This was the beginning of the LDS practice of gathering members at a specific location.

On July 20, 1831, Smith received a revelation in which he was instructed that Independence, in Jackson County, Missouri, was to be the area God had "consecrated for the gathering of the saints . . . and the place for the city of Zion . . . and a spot for the temple."[18] Two months later he received this promise: "Which city shall be built, beginning at the temple lot . . . which temple shall be reared in this generation."[19] To this day, the LDS Church has not built the temple in Independence.

During the next two years the Mormon population in Missouri steadily grew. But trouble was brewing. An LDS source explained the tension: "Local citizens were naturally apprehensive of a religious zeal that predicted that all 'gentiles' [non-Mormons] would be cut off when the millennial kingdom was established in Jackson County."[20]

During this time Smith continued his work on his Bible translation. New revelations gave instructions for establishing the church, including one explaining the different levels of heaven. In 1833 a compilation of Smith's revelations was printed in Independence under the title *A Book of Commandments, for the Government of the Church of Christ*. Before the books could be bound, a mob attacked the print shop and destroyed the press. A small number of copies were salvaged and bound.

At this time many of the Mormons in Jackson County were driven from their homes. In February of 1834, Joseph Smith received a revelation to raise an army to march from Ohio to Missouri to redeem Zion.[21] But his efforts met with failure. Nearly two hundred Mormons made the march of more than one thousand miles, but the whole venture turned into a disaster when the group got bogged down on the edge of Fishing River, Missouri, in a terrible storm. An outbreak of cholera struck more than sixty-five men, with about a dozen dying from the disease.[22]

At the start of the next year Smith called for a meeting to give special recognition to all those who had been a part of the march to Missouri. "President Smith then stated that the meeting had been called, because God had commanded it; and it was made known to him by vision and by the Holy Spirit. . . . And it was the will of God that those who went to Zion, with a determination to lay down their lives, if necessary, should be ordained to the ministry, and go forth to prune the vineyard for the last time, or the coming of the Lord, which was nigh—even fifty-six years should wind up the scene."[23] This prophecy never came true either.

After many appeals to the state government of Missouri, the Mormons were able to obtain permission to have a place to relocate. Finally, in 1836, Caldwell County was created specifically for Mormon settlement to separate them from their non-Mormon neighbors. Far West was made the county seat. Their troubles were not over, however, as more and more Mormons moved into the area and their numbers started to spread into surrounding counties. Non-Mormons began to fear the Mormon voters would control the local government.

In 1835 Joseph Smith brought out a new edition of his revelations. This new edition contained major revisions to already published revelations, added revelations given since the last printing, and added a series of lessons referred to as "Lectures on Faith." This new volume was printed under the title *Doctrine and Covenants of the Church of the Latter Day Saints*.

When this volume was presented to the church for acceptance, most of the members did not know about the alterations that had been made. When knowledge of the changes spread among the members, many were troubled and some left the church. But eventually the leaders convinced the majority that the revisions were acceptable as long as the prophet approved the changes. David Whitmer, one of the witnesses to the *Book of Mormon*, explained the thoughts behind the struggle: "Some of the Latter Day Saints have claimed that God had the same right to authorize Brother Joseph to add to any revelations certain words and facts, that He had to give him any revelations at all: but only those who are trusting in an arm of flesh and are in spiritual blindness, would pretend to make this claim; that God would give his servants some revelations, command them to publish them in His *Book of Commandments,* and then authorize them to change and add to them some words which change and reverse the original meaning: as if God had changed his mind after giving his word. No brethren! God does not change and work in any such manner as this."[24]

One of the new sections added to the 1835 edition of *Doctrine and Covenants* was on marriage. It read in part: "Inasmuch as this church of Christ has been reproached with the crime of fornication, and polygamy: we declare that we believe, that one man should have one wife; and one woman, but one husband, except in case of death, when either is at liberty to marry again."[25] This addition was meant to counter the local gossip that Joseph Smith was having relations with his seventeen-year-old housemaid, Fanny Alger.

There seems to be sufficient evidence that there was a union between them. But was it a secret plural marriage or adultery? Today Mormon historians list Fanny as one of Smith's earliest plural wives.[26] But *Book of Mormon* witness Oliver Cowdery called it something else. Writing to his brother, Warren, in January of 1838, Cowdery expressed his disgust: "When he [Joseph Smith] was there we had some conversation in which in every instance I did not fail to affirm that what I had said was strictly true. A dirty, nasty, filthy affair of his and Fanny Alger's was talked over in which I strictly declared that I had never deviated from the truth in the matter, and as I supposed was admitted by himself."[27]

Joseph Smith's secret polygamy, involving at least thirty-three women, would continue through the rest of his life, always with denials. Smith's polygamy was not publicly acknowledged until 1852, eight years after his death.[28]

Other developments in Kirtland included the calling of twelve apostles, who were then sent on missions. In the summer of 1835, a traveling exhibition of Egyptian mummies and scrolls came to Kirtland. After some negotiations the Mormons were able to purchase the collection. Joseph declared this about the purchase: "I commenced the translation of some of the characters or hieroglyphics, and much to our joy found that one of the rolls contained the writings of Abraham, another the writings of Joseph of Egypt, etc.—a more full account of which will appear in its place, as I proceed to examine or unfold them."[29]

This work was eventually published as part of the Mormon scriptures, *Pearl of Great Price.* The heading of the book reads: "THE BOOK OF ABRAHAM, Translated From The Papyrus, By Joseph Smith. . . . The writings of Abraham while he was in Egypt, called the Book of Abraham, written by his own hand, upon papyrus."[30] Included with the translation were three drawings from the papyri, together with Smith's explanation of the drawings. However, Smith did not foresee the development of Egyptology. Today, Egyptologists have shown that the papyri Smith supposedly translated date to about the time of Christ and are standard Egyptian funeral documents, depicting various Egyptian gods and goddesses.[31] Obviously, these papyri do not relate to the Abraham of the Old Testament, as Joseph Smith claimed.[32]

Even though Kirtland, Ohio, was growing during the 1830s, there were mounting financial problems among the Mormon settlers. The LDS leaders set up several businesses, borrowed heavily from people in the east, speculated in land purchases, built the Kirtland temple, and assisted poor members. But their creditors were growing impatient.

During the summer of 1836, Smith turned once again to treasure hunting to solve the church's financial problems. A member had reported that there was a house in Salem, Massachusetts, with a large fortune hidden in the basement. He believed if Smith would seek the rental of this house, he could unearth the treasure and pay the church's debts. Consequently, Smith, Rigdon, and two others traveled to Salem and rented the house. They had been promised in a revelation that "I have much treasure in this city for you, for the benefit of Zion," that Salem's "gold and silver shall be yours," and "concern not yourselves about your debts, for I will give you power to pay them."[33] Yet no treasure was found, and the church sank even deeper in debt.

Mormon leaders then tried to establish their own bank, but they could not get a state charter. So, instead, they set up the "Kirtland Safety Society Anti-Banking Company." This was something like a nineteenth-century savings and loan, except without a charter and sufficient capital. Richard Van Wagoner explained the attraction: "Mormons accepted Safety Society notes as legal tender because they believed the bank was created by God, that it had a sacred mission, and thus was invincible. Both Rigdon and Smith contributed liberally to the creation of this impression."[34]

Soon the community realized that there was little to back the notes that had been issued. This led to a period of threats, reorganization, and numerous lawsuits against Smith and Rigdon. The venture soon failed.

The effects of the bank's collapse reverberated throughout the whole area of Kirtland. About 15 percent of the Mormons, including some of the top leadership, left the church over this. During the night of January 12, 1838, Smith and Rigdon, fearing both legal action and mobs, fled in secret from Kirtland to the Mormon colony in Far West, Missouri, leaving their families to pack up on their own and follow them.

But the community of Far West held its own set of problems. In residence were several influential former leaders of Smith's church, such as David Whitmer, Oliver Cowdery, and John Whitmer. They cautioned people to be careful about turning over their whole substance to Smith. Fearing the influence of these men, the new Mormon leaders organized a sort of secret church police called the "Danites."

On the Fourth of July 1838, church leaders had a special meeting at the town square. Sidney Rigdon gave a very wild, threatening speech using the text of Matthew 5:13 to denounce the apostates in their midst: "Ye are the salt of the earth: but if the salt have lost his savour, wherewith shall it be salted? it is thenceforth good for nothing, but to be cast out, and to be trodden under foot of men" (KJV). Rigdon continued his threats: "And that mob that comes on us to disturb us, it shall be between us and them a war of extermination."[35]

As the news of Rigdon's speech was circulated throughout the area, non-Mormons became even more angry with their Mormon neighbors. Other problems arose when Mormons tried to vote on August 6, 1838, causing a small riot at Gallatin. Soon pillaging commenced on both sides.

In October, Smith dispatched sixty Mormons to rescue three of their men from the state militia company patrolling the county line. The confrontation became known as the Battle of Crooked River. Although only three Mormons and one man from the state militia died, it was reported to Governor Boggs that the Mormons caused a massacre. This led to Governor Boggs's infamous command on October 27 to General Clark: "The Mormons must be treated as enemies and must be exterminated or driven from the state, if necessary for the public good."[36]

This was followed by the terrible Haun's Mill massacre, where two hundred militiamen attacked the small Mormon settlement. Seventeen men and boys were murdered and fifteen wounded. The women had hidden in the woods when the soldiers approached.

In response to the governor's order, the leaders of the Mormon Church were rounded up by the state militia for trial on charges of treason, murder, arson, burglary, robbery, larceny, and perjury. Meanwhile, the church members were put on standby to surrender their property and leave the state.

Joseph and several others spent the winter in Liberty Jail, in Clay County, awaiting trial. Meanwhile, Brigham Young helped the weary members pool their meager resources to finance the Mormon exodus from Missouri. It is estimated that between twelve thousand and fifteen thousand Mormons left the state.

Finally, in the spring of 1839, a change of venue was arranged for the LDS prisoners. During the move Joseph Smith was able to bribe the local official to allow him and the other LDS prisoners to escape.[37]

THE NAUVOO YEARS

The Mormons fled to the far banks of the Mississippi, to a hamlet called Commerce, Illinois. Here they purchased land to build their new home, renaming it Nauvoo. Though many were sick and poor, they went to work to rebuild their dreams of a city for God's people. With astounding missionary success in England, Mormon immigrants soon helped to swell the numbers in Nauvoo. Joseph's kingdom was finally rising from the dust.

In 1841 Joseph was teaching polygamy to select members and secretly taking plural wives himself. This same year he declared that it was God's will that they build a temple where they could carry out the higher ordinances of the gospel. One of the new revelations announced that by proxy a person could be baptized for a dead loved one and thus open the opportunity for the deceased to enter the highest heaven. He also recruited an army called the Nauvoo Legion with himself as lieutenant general.

In 1842 Smith finished translating the Book of Abraham and published it in the LDS newspaper, *Times and Seasons*. This new scripture contained a different creation story than his earlier Bible revision. Although much of the text was taken from Genesis, there was a new teaching that a plurality of gods created the earth: "And they went down at the beginning, and they, that is the *Gods,* organized and formed the heavens and the earth."[38]

After leading men of the church set up a Masonic lodge in the city, Joseph Smith was admitted and rose to the highest degree. He then began work on his own temple ceremony, incorporating many of the same handshakes, passwords, symbols, and penalties that he had witnessed at the Masonic lodge. Just as he had claimed that Mormonism was the true restoration of the New Testament church, he asserted that his temple ceremony was the restoration of the true ceremony from Solomon's temple, while the Masons had the apostate form.

Then came the publication of *The History of the Saints; or an Expose of Joe Smith and Mormonism,* written by Joseph's former right-hand man, John C. Bennett. This detailed the secrets of polygamy and Smith's use of the Masonic symbols in his temple ceremony. The charges of polygamy always brought forth denials by Smith and the leadership.

In Smith's newest, secret revelation, he supposedly received instructions on the nature of eternal marriage and polygamy. Besides a man's ability to be married in the eternities to his wife, he could add other wives as well. Those that entered these new covenants were promised that they would have "a fulness and a continuation of the seeds [children] forever and ever. Then shall they be gods, because they have no end. . . . Then shall they be gods, because they have all power, and the angels are subject unto them." The revelation went on to command Joseph's wife, Emma, to "receive all those that have been given unto my servant Joseph, and who are virtuous and pure before me; and those who are not pure, and have said they were pure, shall be destroyed, saith the Lord God. . . . And I command mine handmaid Emma Smith, to abide and cleave unto my servant Joseph. . . . But if she will not abide this commandment she shall be destroyed, saith the Lord; for I am the Lord thy God, and will destroy her if she abide not in my law." The revelation then reverted back to a general command: "And again, as pertaining to the law of the priesthood—if any man espouse a virgin, and desire to espouse another, and the first give her consent . . . then is he justified. . . . And if he have ten virgins given unto him by this law, he cannot commit adultery. . . . And again, verily, verily, I say unto you, if any man have a wife, who holds the keys of this power, and he teaches unto her the law of my priesthood, as pertaining to these things, then shall she believe and administer unto him, or she shall be destroyed, saith the Lord your God; for I will destroy her."[39] With such dire warnings, many LDS women felt they could not refuse the new doctrine.

Smith gradually selected the leaders that he felt would be most open to the secret teaching. By the time of his death in 1844, thirty of the leading men of Mormonism had married a total of 114 wives. Only their legal wives were ever publicly acknowledged in Nauvoo.[40]

Another potentially explosive secret was the Council of F˺ Fawn Brodie explained the secret council:

For many years Joseph had talked about building the King-dom of God upon earth, and with his increasing success the idea seems to have been subtly transformed from a mere sym-bol to a thing of substance. As he came more and more to look upon Nauvoo as an autonomous state, the Kingdom of God assumed an unmistakably temporal nature. Finally, in the spring of 1844, Joseph began to organize a government to rule over what he hoped would eventually be a sovereign Mormon state. On March 11 he began selecting with the utmost secrecy a council of fifty "princes" to form what one of them described as "the highest court on earth." Few secrets in Mormon history have been better kept than the activities of this council, but it is clear that one of their first acts was to ordain and crown Joseph as King of the Kingdom of God.[41]

Another development in Nauvoo was Smith's radical teaching on the nature of God. In one of his most famous speeches, he declared his beliefs: "If men do not comprehend the character of God, they do not comprehend themselves. . . . What kind of a being is God? . . . God himself was once as we are now, and is an exalted man, and sits enthroned in yonder heavens! That is the great secret. . . . We have imagined and supposed that God was God from all eternity. I will refute that idea, and take away the veil, so that you may see. . . . God himself, the Father of us all, dwelt on an earth, the same as Jesus Christ Himself did; and I will show it from the Bible."[42]

Two months later, shortly before his death, he preached: "Now you know that of late some malicious and corrupt men have sprung up and apostatized from the Church of Jesus Christ of Lat-ter-day Saints, and they declare that the Prophet believes in a plu-rality of Gods, and, lo and behold! We have discovered a very great secret, they cry—'The Prophet says there are many Gods, and this proves that he has fallen.' I will preach on the plurality of Gods. I have selected this text for that express purpose. I wish to declare I have always and in all congregations when I have preached on the subject of the Deity, it has been the plurality of Gods."[43]

Finally, some of Smith's key men had been pushed too far, asked to accept or overlook too much. Joseph was out of control—teaching strange doctrines and engaging in too many illegal activities. Several pleaded with him to give up these new teachings and practices, but Joseph would not back down. Finally, they set up an opposition newspaper called the *Nauvoo Expositor*. Its one and only issue exposed Smith's secret polygamy teachings and relationships, and his political maneuvers.

Smith, as mayor of Nauvoo, ordered the destruction of the press. The city council then declared that the press was libelous and must be destroyed. The Nauvoo Legion dispatched a group of men to the printing shop to destroy the press and burn all copies of the *Expositor*. This action caused such an outpouring of public condemnation that Smith realized his life was in danger. Soon there was word of a posse coming from Missouri to arrest Smith for crimes committed earlier in that state. Smith, fearing a mob, called out the Nauvoo Legion to protect the city and to prepare for war. His next plan was to escape across the river into Iowa, but Emma pleaded with him that his actions could possibly bring destruction on Nauvoo. Finally, Joseph Smith, his brother Hyrum, and several others surrendered to the county militia at Carthage. All but Joseph and Hyrum were released on bail.

During the next couple of days a few men were allowed to visit them. At some point two guns were smuggled into the jail. Late in the afternoon of June 27, 1844, a mob of about one hundred men stormed the jail. Using the guns that had been smuggled in to them, Joseph and Hyrum tried to defend themselves against the assailants. Within minutes the two brothers lay dead.[44]

THE NEXT PROPHET

At the time of the murders most of the twelve apostles were in the east on missions. It took some time for them to hear of the deaths and to make their way back to Nauvoo. Finally, on Thursday, August 8, 1844, seven of the twelve apostles called for a meeting of the church. Sidney Rigdon presented his claim to be Joseph's successor. Several others offered their views. Brigham Young [1] for the right of the Quorum of Twelve to be in charge. The C of Twelve was given the control of the church. Brigham Y(

president of the quorum, began taking more and more of the church leadership.

Trouble did not end with Joseph's death. The citizens of Illinois still wanted the Mormons to leave. The Mormons were already planning on moving to the west in the spring, but due to a federal indictment that had been issued in January against the top leadership, the date of departure was rescheduled for February 2, 1846. Nine of the LDS apostles were charged with counterfeiting, and to avoid arrest, they fled in the night. The first group to leave Nauvoo had to cross the frozen Mississippi into Iowa.[45]

After spending the winter of 1846–47 at Council Bluffs, Iowa, the Mormons moved west to the Rocky Mountains. Brigham Young looked down into the Salt Lake Valley on July 24, 1847, and announced, "This is the place." Brigham Young was sustained as the second president and prophet of the Mormon Church on December 27, 1847. The Latter-day Saints had found a home and a new prophet. Their Zion would once again rise from the dust.

WITNESSING POINTS

- History reveals that Joseph Smith was involved in occultic practices and multiple "marriages," or adulterous affairs.
- The LDS Church claims to be the only true church on the face of the earth and that all other denominations are wrong.
- The LDS claim to have the only final and true religion contradicts both the Bible and Christian history.
- Mormon doctrines have been changed over time.
- The more sinister and controversial aspects of Mormon history are not known by the average Mormon.
- While it is important to know the controversial elements of Mormon history, they need not take precedence when sharing your faith with LDS. Keep the main and essential doctrines of the gospel, the person and work of Christ, and salvation by grace as the main elements in your witness.

Chapter 4
POLYTHEISM REBORN

Most pagan cultures share a belief in many deities. All through the Old Testament we read of the neighbors of Israel and their pantheon. In the New Testament we read about the apostles' troubles with those who believed in the Greek gods and goddesses.

When Paul encountered the philosophers in Athens, they commented, "He seems to be a proclaimer of foreign gods" (Acts 17:18). Paul responded, "I . . . found an altar with this inscription:

TO THE UNKNOWN GOD.

Therefore, the One whom you worship without knowing, Him I proclaim to you: God, who made the world and everything in it, since He is Lord of heaven and earth, does not dwell in temples made with hands" (Acts 17:23–24).

Paul was not preaching about one god among many, but about the one and only God of the universe.

IS THERE ONE GOD OR MANY?

One of the themes throughout the Bible is that the Creator of the universe, the God of Israel, is the only true God. This is emphasized time after time in the Book of Isaiah: "Before Me there was no God formed, / Nor shall there be after Me" (43:10). "I *am* the First, and I *am* the Last; / Besides Me *there is* no God" (44:6). Yet the fifty-five thousand missionaries sent out each year by the LDS Church are challenging this central biblical theme and its long-held acceptance in Judaism and Christianity. The LDS doctrine of multiple gods is a radical departure from the theistic perspective of Christians and Jews alike.

In the LDS *Articles of Faith* we read, "We believe in God, the Eternal Father, and in His Son, Jesus Christ, and in the Holy Ghost." But a non-Mormon is unlikely to realize that this is a very abbreviated statement of LDS beliefs. The problem lies in what this statement does not say. Mormons believe that the Father, Son, and Holy Spirit are totally separate gods. LDS apostle Bruce R. McConkie explained the concept: "Three separate personages—Father, Son, and Holy Ghost—comprise the Godhead. As each of these persons is *a God*, it is evident, from this standpoint alone, that a *plurality of Gods* exists. To us, speaking in the proper finite sense, these *three* are the only *Gods* we worship. But in addition there is an *infinite number* of holy personages, drawn from worlds without number, who have passed on to exaltation and are thus *Gods*" (emphasis added).[1]

Not only does the LDS Church teach that there are three gods in the godhead but that there are other gods as well. They also believe that God has not always been God. LDS Church leader B. H. Roberts expressed this: "The belief of the Latter-day Saints regarding the personality of God and our relationship to him has been crystallized by President Lorenzo Snow into the aphorism, one of the most expressive in the language: *'As man is, God once was; as God is, man may be.'* No statement could set forth more clearly the nature of God's exaltation and man's destiny."[2]

Every LDS child grows up learning this statement, a statement that is contrary to everything we learn in the Bible about God. If God was once a man on some other world, then there had to be a different god in charge of that world. Most Mormons have never analyzed the implications of this statement.

Both the Old and New Testaments maintain there is only one absolute, holy God, who has never been less than he is today. We read in Habakkuk 1:12, "Are You not from everlasting, O LORD my God, my Holy One?" The psalmist declares, "Your righteousness *is* an everlasting righteousness" (Ps. 119:142).

LDS leaders speak of a time when God was not God but a human on another earth. B. H. Roberts stated, "But if God the Father was *not always God,* but came to his present exalted position by *degrees of progress* as indicated in the teachings of the prophet, how has there been a God from all eternity? The answer is that there has been and there now exists *an endless line of Divine Intelligences—Deities,* stretching back into the eternities, that had no beginning and will have no end. Their existence runs parallel with endless duration, and their dominions are as limitless as boundless space."[3]

Joseph Smith taught that God was once a finite man on another world. In one of his last sermons, Smith preached, "God himself was once *as we are now,* and is an exalted man, . . . it is necessary we should understand the character and being of God and *how he came to be so;* for I am going to tell you how *God came to be God.* We have imagined and supposed that God was God from all eternity. I will refute that idea."[4]

Dr. Sterling M. McMurrin of the University of Utah observed, "In its rejection of the classical concept of God as eternal, Mormonism is a *most radical* digression from traditional theism. This is perhaps its most important departure from familiar Christian orthodoxy, for it would be difficult to overestimate the importance to theology of the doctrine that God is a *temporal* being."[5]

DOES GOD HAVE A BODY?

One of Joseph Smith's revelations says, "God the Father is a glorified and perfected Man, a Personage of flesh and bones."[6] Even though LDS leaders have repeatedly taught that God has a resurrected body, many LDS are not familiar with this teaching. One of their top leaders stated it this way: "So our *Father in heaven* must have gone through a life of mortality and become *resurrected,* and we have to have a Mother in heaven, because we could not have a Father without a Mother at any time, in any life. We were their children born after their resurrection. Before we came on this earth, we were personages of spirit."[7]

Mormons will sometimes try to prove that God has a physical body by pointing to verses in the Old Testament such as Exodus 33:11, "So the LORD spoke to Moses face to face, as a man speaks to his friend." When viewed in context, however, it's clear that this passage is talking about the personal nature of the communication between God and Moses. God spoke to Moses as if he were a friend. The verse does not imply, much less teach, that God has a physical, human-like body. In fact, in verse 9, Moses describes God's presence as a cloudy pillar standing in the door of the tabernacle, and verse 20 says that God told Moses, "You cannot see My face; for no man shall see Me, and live." So whatever Moses saw, it was not a man-like God.

Even if these verses were to be taken literally, they would not help the Mormon argument, since Mormons themselves claim that Jesus is the Jehovah of the Old Testament. They believe that Elohim is God the Father, a totally separate god from Jehovah. Since it is clearly Jehovah who speaks to Moses, His appearance would prove nothing about the Father. To a Christian, however, Jehovah and Elohim are the same God, just different names of the one God. But to a Mormon these names specify completely separate deities. This poses an additional problem for the Mormon argument when we see that the Bible uses the two names together. Moses declared, "Hear, O Israel: The LORD [Jehovah] our God [Elohim] *is* one LORD [Jehovah]" (Deut. 6:4 KJV).

Attributing human characteristics (hands, eyes, ears, etc.) to God in the Bible is called *anthropomorphism*, that is, describing God in physical terms. These verses are not to be taken literally. If verses like Exodus 33:11 teach that God has a physical body, does Psalm 91:4 teach that God has wings, for it says, "Under His [God's] wings you shall take refuge"?

In the New Testament numerous statements show that God does not have a literal body. John declared, "God is Spirit" (John 4:24). Paul referred to Christ as the "image of the invisible God" (Col. 1:15). At another time Paul wrote that God is "invisible" (1 Tim. 1:17), "whom no man has seen or can see" (1 Tim. 6:16). John recorded, "No one has seen God at any time. The only begotten Son, who is in the bosom of the Father, He has declared *Him*" (John 1:18).

In 1843 Smith wrote, "John 14:23—The appearing of the Father and the Son, in that verse, is a personal appearance; and the idea that the Father and the Son *dwell in a man's heart* is an old sectarian notion, and is *false*."[8] This, however, contradicts such verses as Romans 8:9–11 ("His Spirit who dwells in you"); 1 Corinthians 3:16–17 ("you are the temple of God and *that* the Spirit of God dwells in you"); Galatians 4:6 ("God has sent forth the Spirit of His Son into your hearts"); and 1 John 3:24 ("Now he who keeps His commandments abides in Him, and He in him. And by this we know that He abides in us, by the Spirit whom He has given us"). Paul wrote, "Do you not know yourselves, that Jesus Christ is in you?—unless indeed you are disqualified" (2 Cor. 13:5).

DOES GOD HAVE A FATHER?

When describing the multiple gods of Mormonism, Smith declared the Christian understanding of the Trinity a strange doctrine:

> I will preach on the plurality of Gods. . . . The heads of the Gods *appointed one God for us;* and when you take that view of the subject, it sets one free to see all the beauty, holiness and perfection of the Gods. . . . Many men say there is one God; the Father, the Son and the Holy Ghost are only one God. I say that is a strange God anyhow—three in one, and one in

three! It is a curious organization. . . . All are to be crammed into one God, according to sectarianism. It would make the biggest God in all the world. He would be a wonderfully big God—he would be a giant or a monster.

Intelligences exist one above another, so that there is no end to them. . . . If Abraham reasoned thus—If Jesus Christ was the Son of God, and John discovered that *God the Father* of Jesus Christ *had a Father,* you may suppose that *He had a Father* also. Where was there ever a son without a father? And where was there ever a father without first being a son? . . . Jesus said that *the Father wrought precisely in the same way as His Father had done before Him.* As the *Father* had done before? He laid down His life, and took it up the same as *His Father had done before.* He did as He was sent, to lay down His life and take it up again; and then was committed unto Him the keys. I know it is good reasoning.[9]

This strange doctrine that our God was a mortal whose world was governed by a father-god and mother-god, who in turn have mothers and fathers, is repeated throughout the sermons of the LDS Church leaders over the past 150 years. The 1985 LDS priesthood manual quoted President Joseph F. Smith as saying, "Man was born of woman; Christ, the Savior, was born of woman; and God, the Father was born of woman." The manual goes on to quote Brigham Young: "He is our Father—the Father of our spirits—and was *once a man* in mortal flesh as we are. . . . It appears ridiculous to the world, under their darkened and erroneous traditions, that God has once been a *finite being.*"[10] These statements sound amazingly like the doctrines Paul condemned in Romans 1:22-23: "Professing to be wise, they became fools, and changed the glory of the incorruptible God into an image made like corruptible man."

How the first god came into existence is one of the unanswered questions of Mormon theology. For if each God was first conceived as a spirit being by divine parents, then every set of divine parents was also first conceived in the same way. If we followed this conceiving chain back through time, would we ever arrive at the first divine parents? If Mormon doctrine is consistent, then the answer would have to be no. There are no first parents, because every set of parents had parents, as did their parents before them and so on throughout all past time. In philosophy, such a causal chain of being is called an "infinite regress." Each God-to-be was conceived by Gods-who-already-were, and so on and so on into the forever past. The problem with such an infinite regress is that if it is true, no Gods could have ever come to exist.

Consider this: suppose you want to borrow a lawn mower from a neighbor so you can cut your grass. You go next door and ask, "Could I borrow your lawn mower?"

Your neighbor replies, "No, I can't loan you one because I don't own one. I'll ask my neighbor if he has one." So your neighbor goes to his neighbor and asks, "Do you have a lawn mower I can borrow?"

This neighbor answers no as well, stating that he doesn't own one but will see if his neighbor has one he could borrow.

Now if this chain of requests goes on and on to neighbor after neighbor with no one found who owns a lawn mower to loan, you will never get a lawn mower to cut your grass. At some point, someone must be found who owns a lawn mower that can be borrowed. If no such person exists, then you will have to find another way to trim your lawn.

Let's use this illustration to think through the infinite regress of gods in Mormon doctrine. If the gods who now exist got their existence from gods who came before them, and those gods got their existence from gods who preceded them, and so on infinitely into the past, then none of the gods could have ever existed. At some point in the chain, there had to be at least one God who did not get his existence from a previous god. This God would have to be self-existent: that is, his existence would not come from a source outside of him; rather, he must have always existed as the uncaused cause of everything else that exists. He is the one who simply has underived existence to loan. His existence is not borrowed or given to him by someone else. He simply is, eternally and infinitely. He is the fullness of existence throughout all ages past, present, and future. Put another way, he is the God who told Moses, "I AM WHO I AM" (Exod. 3:14), which means that God is the eternally self-existent One, dependent on no one and no thing for his being. When Jesus told his Jewish audience, "before Abraham was, I AM"

MORMONISM UNMASKED

(John 8:58), he was saying that he was the same God who told Moses centuries before, "I AM WHO I AM." The Jews understood this, which is why "they took up stones to throw at him" (John 8:59). They knew that if he was not the one true God, that he had blasphemed and was worthy of death.

Unlike Mormon theology, orthodox Christian doctrine affirms what the Bible teaches: that there is only one God, eternally and infinitely self-existent. He is not a Father or Mother god among many but the only Father God of all. He has no parents. Instead, he is the one who created all else that exists. All other so-called gods are not gods at all, for their existence—assuming they exist at all—is completely dependent on the one God who just has existence to give. "Without Him nothing was made that was made" (John 1:3).

This is why Christians maintain that they believe in and worship the one and only God, the Creator of all, whereas at best, Mormons believe in and worship the creations of Christianity's God. In the apostle Paul's words, Christians believe that the LDS have "exchanged the truth about God for a lie and worshipped and served the creature rather than the Creator, who is blessed forever!" (Rom. 1:25). Given the problems of an infinite regress, it's impossible to see how Mormon theology could escape this criticism and conclusion.

IS GOD MARRIED?

The LDS leaders speak of a particular finite man who entered into an eternal marriage on another world. They teach that after this man and woman died and went to heaven, and after eons of time, they advanced to the point where they were appointed to be god and goddess of our earth. God and his wife procreated the spirits of every person who was or will be born on our earth.

Sometimes LDS people will deny that it is an official doctrine of their church that there is a Heavenly Mother, but this is usually due to ignorance of LDS source material. For instance, in addition to the four books of scripture that LDS members use, there are also statements by their first presidency that are considered authoritative on doctrine. One such statement was made in 1925: "The

Father of Jesus Christ is our Father also. . . . Jesus, however, is the first born among all the sons of God—the first begotten in the spirit, . . . He is our elder brother, and we, like him, are in the image of God. All men and women are in the similitude of the universal Father and Mother, and are literally sons and daughters of Deity."[11] The LDS teach that as spirit beings we all preexisted with God and his wife in heaven before our birth here on earth.

The teaching of a Heavenly Mother raises many questions. LDS insist that exaltation is for men and women together as equals, becoming gods and goddesses of future worlds. This is the reason LDS couples desire a temple wedding, so their union will continue throughout the eternities. Without this eternal marriage they would never have eternal life (the ability to procreate life eternally). They would live in a single state for all eternity.

Yet the woman's role is not one of equality. Her main function is to give birth to the millions of spirits (in the premortal state) needed to populate an earth. When these spirits are sent to an earth to become mortal, they will not pray to her. She will not have a name and will not be mentioned in their scriptures. Whereas the Father will be worshipped, prayed to, and be the main person in their scriptures. This has led a number of LDS women to speak more of the Mother-god and to pray to her.

Speaking at the October LDS conference in 1991, President Hinckley instructed the women of the church: "And now, speaking of prayer, I touch on another matter . . . over which some few women of the Church appear to be greatly exercised. . . . I speak of those who advocate the offering of prayers to our Mother in Heaven. . . . In light of the instruction we have received from the Lord Himself, I regard it as inappropriate for anyone in the Church to pray to our Mother in Heaven. . . . The fact that we do not pray to our Mother in Heaven in no way belittles or denigrates her."[12]

One wonders how Mormons reconcile the existence of a Heavenly Mother with their statement that there are three in the godhead: Father, Son, and Holy Ghost? It would seem that there are four in their godhead: Father, Mother, Son, and Holy Ghost. Regardless, there is nothing in the Bible to indicate that God has a wife. First of all, there is only one God (Deut. 6:4; Mark 12:29).

The godhead is the Father, Son, and Holy Spirit (Matt. 28:19). Obviously, this does not include a wife. God told Isaiah, "Everyone who is called by My name, / Whom I have created for My glory; / I have formed him, yes, I have made him" (Isa. 43:7). And further on he declares, "Thus says the LORD, your Redeemer, / And He who formed you from the womb: / 'I *am* the LORD, who makes all *things*, / Who stretches out the heavens all alone, / Who spreads abroad the earth by Myself" (44:24). Notice that God formed us alone, by himself. God declared, "I *am* the LORD, that *is* My name; / And My glory will I not give to another, / Nor My praise to carved images" (42:8). If God will not share his glory with another, how can there be a goddess Mother in heaven?

ARE WE THE SAME SPECIES?

Included in the teaching that we are all literally spirit children of God is the concept that Jesus and Lucifer are our older brothers. This would also mean we are all the same species, ultimately conceived by the same parental stock that conceived Jesus and Lucifer. Several years ago LDS apostle Joseph F. Merrill confirmed this heritage: "Satan is a person with a spirit body, in form like that of all other men. He is a spirit brother of ours and of our Lord Jesus Christ, who is our Elder Brother in the spirit world."[13] This teaching robs Christ of his deity and brings God down to man's level. As LDS leader B. H. Roberts taught: "What is God? He is a *material intelligence*, possessing both *body and parts*. He is in the form of man, and is in fact of *the same species;* and is a model, or standard of perfection to which man is destined to attain: he being the great Father, and head of the whole family. If we are all the *same species as God*, then the only differences between them [God, Jesus, and Lucifer] and us are time and level of progression."[14]

The LDS Church teaches that we are literally sons and daughters of God and his wife. However, the Bible clearly teaches that we are the children of God by adoption, not by birth. Paul taught that we are children of God by faith (Gal. 3:26). In the Book of Romans, Paul wrote that those who are led by the Spirit are the sons of God and have received the Spirit of adoption (Rom. 8:14–16). He wrote that the children of flesh are not the children of God (Rom. 9:8). John declared that one must believe to be a son of God (John 1:12). Second Corinthians 6:17–18 and 1 John 3:10–11 say much the same thing.

DO MEN BECOME GODS?

Mormonism teaches that man has the potential to become a god over another world in the same sense that God is over this world. In one of Smith's revelations, it is declared that those who inherit eternal life "shall pass by the angels, and the gods, which are set there, to their exaltation . . . . Then shall they be gods, because they have no end."[15] Joseph Smith proclaimed:

> Here, then, is eternal life—to know the only wise and true God; and you have got to *learn how to be Gods yourselves,* . . . To inherit the same power, the same glory and the same exaltation, until you arrive at the station of a God, and ascend the throne of eternal power, the same as those who have gone before. What did Jesus do? . . . *My Father worked out his kingdom with fear and trembling,* and I must do the same; and when I get my kingdom, I shall present it to my Father, so that he may obtain kingdom upon kingdom, and it will exalt him in glory. He will then take a *higher exaltation,* and I will take his place, and thereby become exalted myself.
>
> When you climb up a ladder, you must begin at the bottom and ascend step by step, until you arrive at the top; and so it is with the principles of the Gospel.[16]

The LDS concept of achieving godhood and perfection is similar to a picture of an eternal escalator. As each person steps on the escalator, he advances equally with the others who are in front of him on the stairs but never passes the one in front. The last one to step on the escalator will arrive at the tenth step just as those who got on before him. Thus we see that the LDS do not believe they will achieve equality with Jesus or God the Father, but at some point they can arrive at the level where Jesus is now. In the mean time, Jesus will have moved further up in his exaltation.

DID GOD CREATE OR REORGANIZE?

The LDS Church teaches that matter is eternal. God did not create the world out of nothing but reorganized existing matter into the shape of the world. Joseph Smith stated, "Now, I ask all who hear me, why the learned men who are preaching salvation, say that God created the heavens and the earth out of nothing? The reason is, that they are unlearned in the things of God, and have not the gift of the Holy Ghost."[17] This doctrine is explained in the *Encyclopedia of Mormonism*:

> Moreover, Latter-day Saints understand 'in the beginning' to mean 'in the beginning of our part of the story,' or in the pre-mortal state 'when God began to create our world.' They do not believe in an absolute beginning, for in LDS theology spirit, *matter*, and element are all *eternal*. Creations may progress from lower to higher orders, . . . but *there never was a time when matter did not exist*. Latter-day Saints reject the common idea of an *ex nihilo* creation—that God made everything that exists out of nonexistence. They teach instead that God created everything out of pre-existing but unorganized materials. He organized pre-existing elements to create worlds, and he organized pre-existing intelligence to beget spirits. The spirits of all human beings existed as God's spirit children before their mortal birth on earth.[18]

The Bible, on the other hand, contradicts the Mormon view of origins. The Bible clearly teaches that everything came into being by the creative act of God, not by reorganizing existing matter. The psalmist exclaimed, "By the word of the LORD the heavens were made, / And all the host of them by the breath of His mouth" (Ps. 33:6). The Levites cried out to God, "You have made heaven, / The heaven of heavens, with all their host, / The earth and everything on it, / The seas and all that is in them, / And You preserve them all" (Neh. 9:6).

The apostle John taught that God was before all things: "In the beginning was the Word, and the Word was with God, and the Word was God. He was in the beginning with God. All things were made through Him, and without Him nothing was made that was made" (John 1:1–3).

DOES THE *BOOK OF MORMON* TEACH PLURAL GODS?

One of the curious aspects of Mormonism is that Joseph Smith founded his church on the idea of only one God, not a plurality of Gods. When a Mormon starts talking to someone about the LDS Church, he usually asks the person to read the *Book of Mormon*. This person will usually think that if she reads the *Book of Mormon*, she will have a good understanding of the LDS Church and its beliefs. However, Smith's teachings changed radically over the years. One would need to read Smith's revelations in *Doctrine and Covenants, Pearl of Great Price,* and his sermons to get a more complete presentation of Smith's views.

The *Book of Mormon,* published the same year Smith started his church, teaches only one God (Alma 11:27–39, 44; 2 Nephi 31:21; Mormon 7:7; 3 Nephi 11:27). In fact, the three witnesses to the *Book of Mormon* conclude their testimony with the words, "And the honor be to the Father, and to the Son, and to the Holy Ghost, which is one God." The *Book of Mormon* also teaches that God is a Spirit (Alma 18:26–28; 22:8–11) and can dwell in our hearts (Alma 34:36). As the years passed, Joseph Smith started making a greater distinction between the Father and the Son, eventually asserting that they were separate deities.

Mormons will point to Smith's 1820 vision of God and Christ as proof that he taught all through his life that the Father and Son were separate beings. The *Encyclopedia of Mormonism* states this: "In Church theology, the doctrine of the nature of God is established more clearly by the *First Vision* of the Prophet Joseph Smith than by anything else. Here, Joseph Smith saw for himself that the Father and the Son were *two separate and distinct beings,* each possessing a body. . . . For Latter-day Saints, no theological or philosophical propositions about God can override the primary experience of the Prophet. . . . Latter-day Saints perceive the Father as an exalted Man in the most literal, anthropomorphic terms."[19]

However, Joseph Smith did not publish his account of the first vision until 1842, twenty-two years after the supposed event. Earlier accounts of the vision do not identify both the Father and Son as appearing. The earliest account, handwritten by Joseph Smith, says that Christ appeared, but says nothing about God the Father. Two other times when Smith related his first vision story to people, he stated that angels appeared.[20]

By the end of his life he was preaching, "In the beginning, the head of the Gods called a council of the Gods; and they came together and concocted a plan to create the world and people it."[21] Smith had gone from Christian Trinitarian theism to pagan polytheism.

WHAT ARE THE CURRENT BELIEFS?

Many times when a Christian talks to a LDS friend, the friend will deny that LDS leaders teach that God was not always God and that he had Father-god above him. Witnessing is further hampered when the LDS Church releases confusing statements. Recently the current president of the LDS Church was interviewed in *Time* magazine. The article caught the sense of confusion: "At first, Hinckley seemed to qualify the idea that men could become gods, suggesting that 'it's of course an ideal. It's a hope for a wishful thing,' but later affirmed that 'yes, of course they can.' (He added that women could too, 'as companions to their husbands. They can't conceive a king without a queen.') On whether his church still holds that God the Father was once a man, he sounded uncertain, 'I don't know that we teach it. I don't know that we emphasize it. . . . I understand the philosophical background behind it, but I don't know a lot about it, and I don't think others know a lot about it.'"[22] Yet the teaching that God was not always God is clearly stated in many LDS books.

One of the current LDS student manuals states, "As shown in this chapter, *our Father in heaven* was once a man as we are now, *capable of physical death*. By *obedience* to eternal gospel principles, he *progressed* from one stage of life to another until he *attained* the state that we call exaltation or godhood. In such a condition, *he and our mother in heaven* were empowered to give birth to spirit children whose potential was *equal* to that of their heavenly parents. We are those spirit children."[23]

The Bible, however, speaks of God as eternally existing, not someone who had a mortal birth and then had to learn or achieve something. The Lord declared, "For I *am* God, and not man, / The Holy One in your midst" (Hos. 11:9). Isaiah asks the rhetorical question, "Who has directed the Spirit of the LORD, / Or *as* His counselor has taught Him? / With whom did He take counsel, and *who* instructed Him, / And taught Him in the path of justice? / Who taught Him knowledge, / And showed Him the way of understanding?" (Isa. 40:13–14)

Obviously, the prophets of the Old Testament had no concept of a god above the God of Israel. The psalmist declared, "Great *is* our Lord, and mighty in power; / His understanding *is* infinite" (Ps. 147:5).

DEFINITIONS MATTER

Many converts to Mormonism have not read enough of their church's new literature to grasp how it has departed from the teachings of the Bible. Mormon leaders use the standard words of Christianity but apply different definitions to key terms.

For example, LDS leaders maintain that any number of gods can be equally omnipotent. The Christian's view of God comes from such passages as Nehemiah 9:6: "You alone *are* the LORD; / You have made heaven, / The heaven of heavens, with all their host, / The earth and everything on it, / The seas and all that is in them, / And You preserve them all. / The host of heaven worships You." Deuteronomy 4:39 declares, "The LORD Himself *is* God in heaven above and on the earth beneath; *there is* no other." But Mormons often respond that these verses apply only to our earth. They insist they only pray to one God, but that does not rule out other gods for other worlds. If that were true, though, one wonders why God told Isaiah, "Is there a God beside me? yea, *there is* no God; I know not *any*" (Isa. 44:8 KJV).

As we talk to our Mormon friends, we need to point out that one of the biblical tests of a prophet is whether he teaches the truth about God. The Book of Deuteronomy has a very severe warning about any prophet who would teach a false view of God

(Deut. 13:2,13). This was such a serious issue in the Old Testament that false prophets were to be put to death (Deut. 13:8–10). From the LDS quotes we have just reviewed, it is obvious that their prophets have taught a false god. LDS people insist that they worship the same God as Christians do, yet their description of God certainly does not match the Bible's.

By way of example, I can choose to call my dog a cat due to the similarities between dogs and cats. Both have two ears, a tail, and four legs. However, that does not change the fact that I own a dog, not a cat. In the same way, LDS are free to say their God is the same as the God of the Bible, but are they really talking about the same God? Compare the characteristics of the God of the Bible with the God of Mormonism (see chart on facing page).

Clearly the LDS Church has attached totally different definitions to biblical concepts. Mormons have a God who was once a finite being, who at one time was under the supervision of a different god, and is married to a Heavenly Mother, a Jesus who is our elder brother and a totally separate god. They also teach that the Holy Spirit is also a totally separate god.

Christians who try to witness to their LDS friends will need to listen carefully and ask questions to discover exactly what their friends understand about Mormonism and the Bible. Until Mormons see the greatness and holiness of God, they will have a hard time understanding the magnitude of his love.

In Luke 7:41–43, Jesus told of a certain creditor who forgave two debtors, one owing far more than the other. He then asked Simon, "Which of them will love him more?"

Simon answered, "I suppose the *one* whom he forgave more."

Jesus said he judged right.

Our wonder at God's love and grace is proportional to our comprehension of our true sinfulness. John exclaimed, "In this is love, not that we loved God, but that He loved us and sent His Son *to be* the propitiation for our sins" (1 John 4:10). As long as a person sees himself as a potential god he will never see himself as a lost sinner in need of the grace of the one and only God.

ONE GOD OF THE BIBLE	PLURAL GODS OF MORMONISM
GOD THE FATHER	
Infinite	Finite
Always God	Became God
Absolutely Holy	Achieved Holiness
All Knowing	Achieved Knowledge
Eternally Perfect	Achieved Perfection
All Powerful	Attained Power
Only Creator	One of Many Designers
THE SON	
Eternal	Procreated by God and Wife
Creator	Our Brother
THE HOLY GHOST	
Eternal	Procreated by God and Wife
Creator	A Spirit Brother
HUMANS	
Created on Earth	Same Species as God
Spiritually Adopted Children	Born to God and Wife

WITNESSING POINTS

- Mormonism does not believe in the sole creator God of the Bible.
- Mormonism believes in the God of this world who was once a man.
- Mormonism teaches an infinite number of gods.
- Mormonism teaches that human beings may become gods.
- Mormonism teaches that God is confined to a physical body and is married.
- Demonstrate to Mormons that the LDS Church teaches these notions about God.
- Point out that to disbelieve the Bible's claim to God's sole authority and exclusivity (he is the only God) is to commit idolatry.

Chapter 5

CONFRONTING THE MORMON JESUS

W ill the *real* Mr. Smith please stand up?"
At one time, the above question was one of the most
familiar to the ears of the American public. You may
be old enough to remember the 1960s popular television show where three contestants all claimed to be the
same person, usually someone who had accomplished
something noteworthy. Four celebrity panelists would
quiz the three about their life and accomplishments to
determine the identity of the "real" personality. The two
impostors purposely lied, wanting to fool the celebrities
into thinking they were the actual person.

After a few minutes of interrogation the panelists voted for the person they thought was telling the truth. Finally, the moderator asked the truthful person to stand. It was all great fun, and the contestants were rewarded monetarily for every vote they received, right or wrong. The program was especially entertaining on the rare occasions when the celebrity panelists were completely stumped and cast all four votes for the wrong contestants.

This old game show illustrates a troubling fact that none of us should forget: It is often difficult to discern truth from falsehood, especially when people put on a convincing disguise and represent themselves as authentic.

Consider a different example. As a college student, I worked as a teller in a national bank. I counted so many thousands of dollars in coins and bills that I became keenly sensitive to the texture of money. On one occasion I was rapidly counting a stack of dollar bills when I felt something out of whack. I carefully examined one particular bill that looked good but felt strange. Sure enough, under close scrutiny, the bill was found to be counterfeit. A casual observer, or one not so used to handling money, was unable to distinguish between a real bill and the fake. On the surface they looked identical. Apparently a teller who was not knowledgeable or skilled enough to spot a counterfeit had accepted the phony money.

The point is that things, ideas, or even people can look authentic on the surface only to be counterfeits in reality. Sometimes we need to look carefully below the surface to find the true substance. This point is no less true in the area of religion. Many ideas, doctrines, and teachers present themselves as Christian, yet their superficial image may mask underlying non-Christian worldviews, deviant doctrinal positions, or outright fraud.

One significant theological tenet where this deceit often appears is that regarding the person and work of Jesus Christ. This is the area of study theologians call Christology. It is rare to find anyone who will not say, "I believe in Jesus." The problem is that this affirmation does not tell us *what* they believe about Jesus, or even what Jesus they believe in. Even most overtly non-Christian religions usually have some place of prominence for Jesus Christ in their system. For example, Muslims regard Jesus as one of the greatest prophets who ever lived, but they do not believe he is the Son of God. Many Hindus acknowledge that Jesus was a great guru or *avatar* (incarnation of deity), but they do not believe he was unique since there have been thousands of such incarnations. Even most atheists are reluctant to demean Jesus. They frequently grant that he was at least "a great moral teacher."

But what about Mormons? What do the LDS believe about Jesus Christ? There is no question that the LDS Church regards itself as a legitimate form of Christianity (in fact, the restored and truest form of Christianity). Also, there is no question that Mormons affirm the historical validity of the birth, life, death, and resurrection of Jesus of Nazareth. They often refer to Jesus as their Savior, as their Lord, as the Son of God, and even as God incarnate as man. Artists' renderings of Jesus adorn LDS visitors centers, ward buildings, offices, homes, and literature. Mormons point with pride to their church's logo, which is emblazoned with the name Jesus Christ as its most prominent feature.

The Church of
Jesus Christ
of Latter-day Saints

There is no doubt that LDS claim Jesus Christ is the central figure in their theology and daily living. And, admittedly, the casual observer would be hard put to find any reason to question the authenticity of that claim, since the name and likeness of Jesus appears consistently in Mormon religious culture. However, like the fake contestants in the old game show who claimed to be who they were not, in some cases pretending so well as to fool four intelligent people, we must ask, *Is the Jesus Christ of Mormonism the real Jesus of the Bible?* In other words, Will the *real* Jesus please stand up? Will he be the Jesus Christ of the Church of Jesus Christ of Latter-day Saints? Here we'll examine the stated teachings of the LDS Church about Jesus Christ, including his preexistence, birth, early life, suffering, death on the cross, resurrection from the dead, and ascension and present status. We will then compare the Mormon view to the one taught in the Bible and affirmed in historic Christianity by every Christian denomination since the New Testament era.

THE PREEXISTENCE
AND DEITY OF CHRIST

The LDS Church teaches that Jesus Christ preexisted prior to his birth on earth. He existed as a spirit Son of a heavenly Father and a heavenly Mother. In that pre-earth world, Jesus, who was called Jehovah, was literally procreated by his heavenly parents into a spiritual realm where he had a familial relationship with them.

According to Mormonism, this was *not* an unusual circumstance, for LDS doctrine says all human beings were the preexistent offspring of God and his wife. *All* people were procreated in a preexistent life before life on earth.[1] Thus, Jesus was not, in that sense, unique among men. His origin was exactly the same as every other human or angel (which are of the same species as people) who has ever lived on earth or heaven, or ever will. He is *a* son of God, but, in this regard, no less or more so than anyone else. Joseph Smith applied this reasoning to himself: "And now, verily I say unto you, I was in the beginning with the Father, and am the Firstborn; And all those who are begotten through me are partakers of the glory of the same, and are the church of the Firstborn."[2]

Incidentally, another of God's sons was Lucifer, who, along with one-third of God's spirit children, waged a great war against their divine parents.[3] The only difference in Jesus' pre-life birth and early life from that of any other person is that Mormonism refers to him as the heavenly Father's "first born" son.[4] This seems to mean that he was the first, chronologically, of all God's children to be born in preexistence. Thus, Mormons refer to Jesus respectfully as their "elder brother." They use the term *literally*, since they believe we are literally his younger siblings. Jesus is "the same species" as God the heavenly Father, but so then are all other people.

Nevertheless, it is implied in Mormon teaching that Jesus did attain, while in his pre-earth existence, a level of divinity. Thus, Mormons claim that Jesus in his preexistence was part of the godhead along with the heavenly Father and the Holy Ghost.[5]

It is clear, however, that Mormons regard the three members of the godhead as totally separate entities. They are united only in purpose and love, not in essence. In other words, they are three different gods (see chap. 4). As *Doctrine and Covenants* states, "The Father has a body of flesh and bones as tangible as man's; the Son also; but the Holy Ghost has not a body of flesh and bones, but is a personage of the Spirit."[6]

What is unclear, however, is exactly how Mormons explain the way Jesus, or the Holy Ghost, achieved deity in the preexistence. Apparently they did so without first having received bodies of flesh and bone, as did the heavenly Father and all other gods before them. This makes Jesus and the Holy Ghost exceptions to what the LDS church teaches is the universal norm: no one can become a god without first becoming an embodied, physical being. No flesh-and-blood body, no achievement of godhood possible. Just how Jesus and the Spirit managed to bypass this requirement has never been explained in LDS literature.

So how does the LDS view compare with the teaching of historic Christianity? The traditional biblical perspective is that Jesus did preexist as the eternal Word (John 1:1), the one and only Son of God. In that preexistence he was always fully and equally God, sharing the same divine essence with the Father and the Holy Spirit. This orthodox view of the godhead maintains that the three Persons of the Trinity comprise the one eternal God. Only *one* God eternally exists in three Persons.

Jesus possesses all of the nature and attributes of God. He is, by definition, then, infinite, eternal, omniscient, omnipresent, omnipotent, and all the other attributes ascribed to deity. The orthodox view is that he is the "firstborn over all creation" (Col. 1:15), which is understood to mean that he is the preeminent ruler of all the universe. He is neither a created being, as some non-Trinitarians assert, nor the oldest procreated child of God, as Mormons claim. He is begotten of the Father from all eternity. Thus he did not have a chronological beginning, since he is not limited to either time or space. He was, is, and in all ways will be God (John 1:1–18; 8:56–59; Phil. 2:6–11; Col. 1:13–22; Heb. 1:3; 13:8).

Needless to say, this is not an easy concept to comprehend, even for trained theologians. Nevertheless, it is the revealed truth about Jesus as derived from the pages of the Bible and it has been affirmed by every Christian tradition—Catholic, Orthodox, and Protestant—since the New Testament era. It is a foundational doctrine of Christianity, and it is not negotiable.

Occasionally, Mormons (as well as other non-Trinitarians) will argue that the orthodox view is not biblical. They frequently argue that it actually reflects the influence of pagan philosophy on the early creeds, which they maintain were forced on the early church by corrupt pagan Roman emperors and church councils. Mormons call this corruption the Great Apostasy.[7] Former LDS president Spencer W. Kimball described it this way: "This is not a continuous church, nor is it one that has been reformed or redeemed. It has been restored after it was lost. It was lost—the gospel with its powers and blessings—sometime after the Savior's crucifixion and the loss of his apostles. The laws were changed, the ordinances were changed, and the everlasting covenant was broken that the Lord Jesus Christ gave to his people in those days."[8]

The truth is that this accusation against historic Christian orthodoxy is illegitimate. The basic doctrines of the full deity of Christ and the Trinity are firmly rooted in biblical evidence and were attested by the earliest church fathers long before the church councils formulated the early creeds.

Here rests, perhaps, the most important single error of the Church of Jesus Christ of Latter-day Saints. They have reduced Jesus from his deserved status as the infinite and eternal Son of God, meaning the Second Person of the Trinity, to that of just another preexistent, finite, and procreated child of the heavenly Father (himself a finite being). In Mormonism, Jesus is, in essence, no different from you and me. Unfortunately, most Mormons seem unable or unwilling to see how radically deviant their view of Jesus is and how much it distorts the essence of Christianity. Christianity rests totally on the premise that God Almighty was in Jesus, who came to earth as a man. This premise forces us to investigate another important dimension of who Jesus is in Mormonism.

THE INCARNATION
AND BIRTH OF CHRIST

Perhaps no biblical teaching has generated more ridicule and scorn from skeptics than has the Christian doctrine of the virgin birth of Jesus. Even many so-called Christians have questioned its validity. It should not surprise us that people doubt its truth; after all, even Mary herself found it hard to believe (Luke 1:34).

We must admit that the event we call the "virgin birth" might better be termed the "virgin conception." It actually refers to Jesus' miraculous fertilization in the womb of Mary by the Holy Spirit, not to his later delivery or birth in Bethlehem (which the *Book of Mormon* states was in Jerusalem, see Alma 7:10). Even granting this, however, the doctrine is taught as a fact in the birth narratives in the Gospels of Matthew and Luke. Bible-believing Christians regard the virgin conception as one miraculous (thus unexplainable) component of the greatest miracle and doctrine of all—the incarnation of God in Christ.

For Christians, there is no more basic and fundamental belief than that the eternal God of the universe, in the Second Person of the Trinity, was born into the material world as a man. Thus Jesus Christ was the God-man, fully human, yet fully divine. All of what historic Christianity purports to be rests on this truth. Granted, I have never met a sincere Mormon who would say he or she did not believe in the virgin birth of Christ. Most LDS literature and public relations information seem to affirm the basic details of Jesus' birth and life as described in the New Testament. For instance, one short film produced by the LDS that dramatizes the birth of Jesus uses no spoken words, only music and images. The birth story looks biblically accurate and is presented in a beautiful and powerful way. So, superficially, it seems that the LDS Church teaches the traditional view of Christ's miraculous birth and incarnation. However, a closer examination of several aspects of Mormon doctrine reveals a much different and, for Bible-believing Christians, disturbing version of this tenet.

To begin with, we must keep in mind the preexistent nature of Christ in LDS theology. Remember, LDS theology teaches that

Jesus was no different essentially than any other human child of God. Rather, Jesus was supposedly just older and more advanced. So his being birthed into earth-life was no different from any other person leaving behind their premortal home to be incarnated into a body of flesh on earth. So why then would Mormons still regard the birth of Christ as unique or miraculous? The answer lies in the Mormon description of the conception itself.

Traditional Christianity, following biblical teaching (Matt. 1:18; Luke 1:35), states that Jesus was conceived in Mary's womb by the Holy Spirit and that Mary remained virginal throughout the entire process until after she delivered him. Mormonism, however, has a different explanation. According to authoritative LDS teachings, Jesus was conceived, not by the Holy Spirit, but by a special physical visitation of God the heavenly Father to earth. LDS teach that the Father had physical, sexual relations with Mary, causing her to conceive the child Jesus. This is why Jesus is referred to in Mormon parlance as the "only-begotten of the Father," a phrase they mean quite literally. One prominent Mormon writer described the event like this: "All men (Christ included) were born as the sons of God in the spirit, one man (Christ only) was born as the Son of God in this mortal world. He is the only begotten in the flesh. God was his Father; Mary was his mother. His Father was an immortal man; his mother a mortal woman. He is the Son of God in the same literal, full, and complete sense in which he is the Son of Mary. There is nothing symbolic or figurative about it."[9] Another prominent LDS theologian said, "Jesus had forty-six chromosomes. Twenty-three came from Mary, and twenty-three came from God the Eternal Father."[10] Former LDS president Joseph Fielding Smith stated it this way: "Our Father in heaven is the Father of Jesus Christ, both in the spirit and in the flesh. Our Savior is the First born in the spirit, the Only Begotten in the flesh. . . . He (Jesus) did not teach them that he was the Son of the Holy Ghost, but the Son of the Father."[11]

This description of the doctrine of the virgin birth sounds strange to Bible-believing Christians, and its implications are staggering. First, the LDS view that the Father conceived Jesus clearly contradicts biblical teaching (and, ironically, *Book of Mormon* teaching [Alma 7:10]). The Bible says Jesus was conceived of the Holy Spirit, not of the Father. Second, and perhaps even more troubling, is the notion that Jesus' conception involved a physical/ sexual union of the heavenly Father and Mary. It is not surprising, therefore, to find that Mormons are particularly reluctant to discuss this doctrine. And when they do, they use various explanations for how exactly this conception may have happened. One Mormon speculated that Jesus could have been a "test tube" conception. Others are more willing to face up to their church's teaching that there was a sexual relationship between God and Mary, but they deny that there was any sort of moral conflict involved in the union, especially since the Father and Mary were not married, and she was betrothed to Joseph, while the heavenly Father was also married to a heavenly Mother. Some Mormons claim that the sexual relationship between Mary and the Father was somehow exempted from normal moral standards. Most Mormons, however, simply shrug and admit they just do not know how the Father impregnated Mary.

The truth is that Mormons cannot escape the sordid implications of their view of Jesus' conception. If, as Mormonism certainly teaches, God the heavenly Father is a being of flesh and bone and possesses a sexual nature, then one is inexorably led to the conclusion that Jesus' conception involved some kind of sexual component. LDS attempts to dispel the obvious moral difficulties seem to demonstrate their own ambivalence and embarrassment to this side of Mormon theology.

Therefore, we must honestly ask, does not the LDS view at least imply that God, the heavenly Father, experienced a sexual arousal and performed physical sex with Mary? Does it not, at least, seem that God had sexual relations with his own spirit-daughter, making him appear guilty of incest? Many Mormons would regard those questions as offensive, as well they should, but until they can offer credible answers to such questions, they must face the unavoidable implications of their unbiblical version of Jesus' conception and birth.

THE LIFE, DEATH, AND
RESURRECTION OF CHRIST

As indicated previously, the LDS Church generally adheres to the traditional details of the life of Jesus as described in the New Testament Gospels of Matthew, Mark, Luke, and John. There are significant differences with historic Christianity, however, in the LDS interpretation of some of the events. For example, the meaning of the events surrounding Jesus' crucifixion is most important. As stated before, Mormons affirm the death and resurrection of Christ as an essential element in their doctrine of the atonement (see chap. 6). Nevertheless, they tend to place a greater degree of importance on Jesus' emotional suffering in the garden of Gethsemane than on his physical death on the cross.[12] This may explain why LDS Church buildings and temples traditionally do not include crosses or crucifixes on their steeples, spires, or walls. Mormons also do not normally wear jewelry with crosses or crucifixes attached. Consider Joseph Fielding Smith's description of the atoning work of Christ:

> We get into the habit of thinking, I suppose, that this great suffering was when he was nailed on the cross by his hands and his feet and was left there to suffer until he died. As excruciating as that pain was, that was not the greatest suffering he had to undergo, for in some way which I cannot understand, but which I accept on faith . . . was our Savior and Redeemer of a fallen world, and so great was his suffering before he ever went to the cross we are informed, that blood oozed from the pores of his body, and he prayed to his Father that the cup might pass if it were possible, but not being possible he was willing to drink.[13]

Mormons also affirm the biblical records concerning the bodily resurrection of Christ. One crucial difference between Mormonism and Christianity, however, is that the LDS teach that Jesus not only appeared to his disciples in Palestine, as recorded in the New Testament, but also to Nephites and Lamanites in the New World as recorded in the *Book of Mormon*.[14] This additional information concerning the life and teachings of Jesus is one reason the LDS Church now gives the *Book of Mormon* the subtitle *Another Testament of Jesus Christ.* Mormons argue that this additional record of Jesus' resurrection is further evidence for his claims to be Savior and Lord (as they understand those terms). Chapter 7 examines the *Book of Mormon's* origin, contents, and history. We will see that LDS claims for that book, and the events about Jesus recorded in it, are untenable.

One final aspect of LDS Christology needs our attention. Mormons assert that following Jesus' resurrection and visitation in the western hemisphere, he ascended into heaven where he now sits at "the right hand of the Heavenly Father." Mormons do not understand that phrase in a figurative or metaphorical sense of prominence within the Trinity, as do all orthodox Christian churches. Rather, Mormons contend that since God the Father is an exalted man of flesh and bone and Jesus is his literal Son, it makes good sense to believe the phrase quite literally. God actually sits on a throne, and Jesus sits beside Him. In fact, Mormons sometimes use this phrase as proof for their doctrine.

NOT THE REAL JESUS

"The votes are in. Will the real Jesus please stand up!" Based on our evaluation and comparison with biblical teaching, the Jesus of Mormonism cannot stand. In 2 Corinthians 11:4, the apostle Paul warned of those who follow "another," or "different" Jesus. The LDS Church asserts that it is a Christian church. Now, more than ever, the name Jesus Christ is prominent on its logo and on most of its literature and buildings. Yet, the inescapable conclusion, based on official LDS statements, is that it does not believe in or proclaim the same Jesus as do Bible-believing Christians. The Mormon Jesus is a different Jesus. If theological and doctrinal beliefs have any bearing on the truth or falsehood of a faith, then we must conclude that Mormonism stands outside the parameters of orthodox, historic Christianity.

WITNESSING POINTS

As we've seen, most Mormons claim to be Christians, to believe in Jesus Christ as Savior, and may even claim to be born again. However, keep the six key points below in mind when addressing their view of Jesus.

- There are critical differences between Mormonism and Christianity on the matter of the preexistent life and deity of Christ. Mormons regard Jesus as their "elder brother," the oldest of the heavenly Father's spirit children who attained godhood. Christianity, on the other hand, says Jesus was God the Son from all eternity, the Second Person of the Trinity and, thus, possesses all attributes of deity.

- Christians can confidently say that the doctrines of the full deity of Christ and the Trinity are firmly grounded in biblical evidence. Some Mormons may argue that Trinitarian theology is unbiblical and based on pagan interpretations. Consider, however, the following examples where Jesus' deity and unity with the Father are affirmed. In response to Philip's request to see the Father, Jesus replied, "Don't you know me, Philip, even after I have been among you such a long time? Anyone who has seen me has seen the Father. How can you say 'Show us the Father'? Don't you believe that I am in the Father, and that the Father is in me? The words I say to you are not just my own. Rather, it is the Father, living in me, who is doing his work" (John 14:9–10 NIV). Also, Jesus forthrightly declared his unity with God: "I and the Father are one" (John 10:30 NIV).

- Though the term *Trinity* does not appear in the Bible, the New Testament clearly links Father, Son, and Holy Spirit together in a Trinitarian way. For instance, in his famous Great Commission passage, Jesus commanded, "Therefore go and make disciples of all nations, baptizing them in the name [singular, not names as if they were separate beings] of the Father and of the Son and of the Holy Spirit" (Matt. 28:19 NIV). The apostle Paul referenced all three divine Persons in the same context of unity when writing about spiritual gifts: "There are different kinds of gifts, but the same *Spirit*. There are different kinds of service, but the same *Lord*. There are different kinds of working, but the same *God* works all of them in all men" (1 Cor. 12:4–6 NIV, emphasis added). Other clearly Trinitarian passages include 2 Corinthians 13:14; Ephesians 4:4-6; and Titus 3:4-6.

- Christians assert that Jesus was conceived miraculously by the Holy Spirit and that the conception involved no sexual or physical component. Mormons, however, maintain that he was the literal offspring of a physical union (implying a sexual relationship) of the heavenly Father and Mary. We must sensitively challenge Mormon assumptions and point to the biblical record of the events surrounding the birth of Christ. Mormons may be surprised to hear our objections to their view and may even be offended when we point out its implications.

- Even the *Book of Mormon* affirms that Jesus was conceived by the Holy Spirit, not the Father (Alma 7:10). This may indicate that Joseph Smith's views were closer to orthodoxy when he first published the *Book of Mormon* (1830).

- It may by difficult for our Mormon friends to acknowledge their church's divergences from Christian orthodoxy. Nonetheless, we must, in love, tell them that we reject the Mormon concept of Jesus as a counterfeit. We must lovingly tell them that if they continue to hold to such views, they are in spiritual danger. Only the real Jesus of the Bible can offer and provide the atonement from sin necessary for salvation. We must put our faith and trust in him as our personal Savior and Lord, not in a different Jesus who has no position or power to save.

Chapter 6
THIS IS GOOD NEWS?

E very religion addresses the human cry for deliverance, restoration, and peace. For orthodox Christians, this issue can be raised with the question, "How may I go to heaven when I die?" Mormonism is no different. Like Christianity, Mormonism accepts the need for salvation and the existence of an afterlife. As we'll see, however, the differences between orthodox Christian theology and LDS teaching on these issues are critical and irreconcilable. Both perspectives cannot be true. If one is right, the other must be wrong.

Before we explore these differences, keep three things in mind: First, Mormonism looks and sounds a lot like Christianity, but the similarities are superficial. Even key terms such as *gospel, eternal life,* and *the Fall* have very different meanings between the two viewpoints. Second, Mormonism insists that a person conforms to its teachings and demands to receive the greatest blessings in the afterlife. Third, Mormonism teaches that almost everyone will go to a better place in the afterlife, even without faith and repentance.

MORMONISM AND THE GOSPEL

People often ask, "Is Mormonism a cult? Does it teach a different gospel?"

Ever since its beginnings, the Church of Jesus Christ of Latter-day Saints claimed the *Book of Mormon* held "*the fulness* of the everlasting gospel."[1] Joseph Smith maintained in his very first recorded "revelation" in *Doctrine and Covenants* that God had spoken to him declaring that God's "everlasting covenant might be established that *the fulness* of my gospel might be proclaimed . . . unto the ends of the world."[2] But Smith's gospel was not the same good news of Jesus Christ, God incarnate, who died on the cross for the sins of the world, securing salvation.

Mormonism teaches that the true gospel was corrupted and lost from the earth when Christ and his apostles died. As Mormon leader and church president Spencer Kimball said, "It was lost, the gospel with its powers and blessings—sometime after the Savior's crucifixion and the loss of his apostles. The laws were changed, the ordinances were changed, and the everlasting covenant was broken that the Lord gave to his people."[3]

According to Mormonism, during the period between roughly A.D. 100 and 1820, when, according to Smith's testimony, God appeared to him, no one knew the "purpose of life" and "the priesthood and revelation were no longer on the earth." In addition there were no God-ordained leaders, apostles, priesthood leaders, or prophets with genuine spiritual gifts and power. The church with all of the saints of God throughout seventeen hundred years of church history—the church that Jesus had promised would not be destroyed (Matt. 16:13–20)—was, according to Mormonism, "the Church of Jesus Christ no longer; it was a church of men."[4]

Mormonism makes two great fallacies at this point. First, it states that its teachings are the same as those of the early church, thus it has restored God's truth on earth. As we have seen in earlier chapters, however, Mormonism is a new religion. Its doctrines, rites, rituals, the office of its prophet, and the importance of its temples are based more on the Freemasons of the 1600s and 1700s than New Testament Christianity, much less Old Testament Judaism.

The second fallacy regarding Mormonism's claim about the "Great Apostasy" is that the Bible and the saving gospel contained within it totally disappeared. (See fig. 6.1.) How can that be when the Bible was present with the church from its inception? The Old Testament, or Hebrew Scriptures, was used by the early apostles when they preached about Christ. The New Testament seemed to come simultaneously into being with the church itself and was completed at least by A.D. 100. Although the church experienced heresies, corruptions, religious wars, and various scandals, it was the Bible and its unchanging truths that brought revival and renewal to the church and the world. In fact, the Protestant Reformation of the sixteenth century came about as a result of a return to Scripture alone as the foundation of truth. Even at the time of the formation of the LDS Church (April 6, 1830), William Carey's Christian missionary movement had already begun. Carey's efforts arguably became the greatest missionary movement of all time, creating "the great century" of gospel advance throughout much of Africa and Asia.

All of this, Mormonism claims, was based on a false—or at best, an incomplete—gospel and was led by an apostate or false church. Mormonism says that it has the only true and full gospel and that all other expressions of the gospel are wrong. To prove their point, Mormons cite Joseph Smith's vision when he asked God which church he should join. "Join none of them," was the response, "for they are all wrong; their creeds are an abomination in my sight and all of their professors [members] are corrupt."[5]

This appearance of God and Jesus to Joseph Smith was the first step in the gospel being restored, Mormonism claims. Later Joseph

THE GREAT APOSTASY ACCORDING TO MORMONISM

CONFESSIONS

Apostle's Creed
Nicea
Chalcedon
Heidelberg
Westminster
All Baptist
  confessions
All Protestant
  confessions

PEOPLE

Augustine
St. Francis
Aquinas
Martin Luther
John Bunyan
William Carey

DENOMINATIONS

Lutheran
Anglican
Presbyterian
Baptist
Evangelical
Catholic

- The first vision of God to Joseph Smith (Spring 1820)
- Publication of the *Book of Mormon* (1830)
- True church is restored as the Church of Jesus Christ of Latter-day Saints (April 6, 1830)

All other denominations continue as incomplete and wrong religious movements.

CIRCA
A.D. 90

A.D. 30

The Church exists; Jesus and the apostles guarantee its validity

With the death of Jesus and the apostles, the Church disappears, and doctrines and practices are lost. Truth and the way of salvation are lost from the earth. According to Morminism, priesthood authorities disappear along with temple ceremonies, "plain and precious" parts of the Bible, and genuine Christianity. The Bible is corrupted. The gospel is lost from the earth.

Figure 6.1

79

was allegedly visited not only by Moroni, a "resurrected being" who showed him the golden plates, but also by John the Baptist, who bestowed on him and his colleague Oliver Cowdery the "Aaronic Priesthood" and its authority.[6] Then came a visit from the apostles Peter, James, and John, who gave to Joseph "the keys of the greater priesthood and their power that the church could be organized on the earth."[7]

All of these visits endowed Smith and his church, according to his interpretation and his account of the events, to practice gospel ordinances, to organize the priesthoods of the church, and to build the temples for the secret and sacred rites of Mormonism. Smith maintained that the power of the gospel had once again been restored to the earth as "the gospel of repentance, and of baptism by immersion for the remission of sins."[8]

Mormonism lays claim, therefore, to possessing the only true and full gospel on the earth. The truth, however, is that it is a gospel that is false and synthetic.

MORMONISM AND HUMANITY

The Christian gospel responds to a need: the desperate plight of the human race that, although created in God's perfect moral image, has fallen short of his righteousness and purity.[9]

In the garden of Eden, Adam and Eve deliberately chose to disobey God's command not to eat of the tree of good and evil. When they chose to disobey him, they fell. They lost their innocence, they were tainted by evil, and their relationship to God was broken. Henceforth, a fallen nature and a natural inclination to sin would be passed on through all the human race.

Jesus Christ was the only person never to have sinned, and that was because he was *Immanuel*, or God with us. He was both God and man. Excepting Jesus, every person stands in need of God's grace and forgiveness.

How does Mormonism view the human race and the nature of the Fall and of sin itself? It is a different analysis from Bible-based Christianity, as we shall see.

The Origin of Humans

First of all, Mormonism does not believe that human life begins with conception in the womb. Rather, spirit and matter, it is argued, have existed from eternity: "The doctrine has prevailed that matter was created out of nothing, but the Lord declares that the elements are eternal. Matter always did and . . . always will exist. . . . We discover . . . that the intelligent part of man was not created, but always existed. It is expressed in several revelations, that man was in the beginning with God . . . however, man was a spirit unembodied." [10]

These spirits took on spirit bodies when they were born as the literal spiritual children of the heavenly Father prior to being born on earth to earthly, physical parents. During the time of their preexistence, these spirits did not possess actual, physical bodies. "These spirit beings, the offspring of exalted parents, were men and women, appearing in all respects as mortal persons do, excepting only that their spirit bodies were made of a more pure and refined substance than the elements from which mortal bodies are made." [11]

If these premortal spirit beings performed well and supported the heavenly Father and Jesus Christ in their struggle against Satan, then they were guaranteed a life of spiritual and general success on this earth. If they did not perform well, they were condemned to a less than prosperous spiritual and earthly journey. "Our place in this world would then be determined by our own advancement or condition in the pre-mortal state, just as our place in our future existence will be determined by what we do here in mortality.

"When therefore, the creator said to Abraham, and to others of his attainment, 'you I will make my rulers,' there could exist no feeling of envy or jealousy among the million other spirits, for those who were 'good and great' were but receiving their just reward." [12]

This idea of a previous spirit life must be accepted on blind faith because Mormonism argues that no memory of the preexistence of spirits lingers now within human beings themselves. As Bruce McConkie has stated, "The probationary nature of our mortal estate calls for us to forget the life we lived and the experiences we had when we dwelt in the courts of the Eternal King." [13]

The Nature of the Fall

Mormonism claims that we had a preexistence as God's literal spirit children. Does that idea agree with Christianity's view that humankind has fallen and needs a savior and salvation? To answer that question, we must look at the experience of Adam and Eve, according to the teachings of the LDS Church.

Like all humankind, Adam, Mormons claim, had a preexistence. But his was as Michael the Archangel, or "the ancient of days."[14] In this sense he and Eve existed as purely spiritual beings although living on the earth. As a result of eating the fruit of the tree of good and evil, both Adam and Eve lost their purely "spiritual state" and became physical beings (2 Nephi 2:22; Moses 3:5–7). The Bible, on the other hand, says that God originally created Adam and Eve from material substance (Adam from the dust of the ground and Eve from one of Adam's ribs), thereby teaching that the first human couple were literal physical beings. The Bible also states that they were created male and female from the beginning, showing that they were sexually defined and differentiated.

At first glance, Mormon thought on the Fall seems similar to Christianity's view. Mormon scriptures tell that Adam and Eve broke God's command not to eat of the tree. On further examination, however, Mormon theology shows itself in conflict with the Bible's declaration that Adam and Eve fell out of God's will. As one Mormon authority stated: "The Lord gave two conflicting commandments—one to become mortal and have children, the other to not eat of the tree of knowledge of good and evil out of which mortality and children and death would result. . . . (Adam) chose to partake of the forbidden fruit so that the purposes of God might be accomplished."[15]

By having eaten of the tree, Adam and Eve actually fulfilled the will of God, contrary to what the Bible states, and were able to have children. Mormon thinkers speak of Adam and Eve as therefore fulfilling God's will, not having sinned at all. "I'm very, very grateful that in the *Book of Mormon*, and I think elsewhere in our scriptures the fall of Adam has not been called a sin. It wasn't a sin. . . . What did Adam do? The very thing the Lord wanted him to do."[16]

So, according to LDS teaching, Adam and Eve choose the good path and became mortal persons so they could have children and advance to godhood in the celestial kingdom. Childbearing is a necessary part of the process toward Mormon exaltation, and without physical bodies, Adam and Eve would have been unable to conceive children of flesh and bone.

While placing childbearing into the plan of salvation, Mormonism has at the same time created a two-faced God who desired the sin of Adam and Eve but punished them with death and separation from him as a result of their sin. Some Mormon thinkers actually praise Adam for his disobedience: "Adam was one of the greatest men who ever lived on the earth. . . . Adam fell, but he fell in the right direction. He fell toward the goal. . . . Adam fell, but he fell upward."[17]

The errors of Mormonism become increasingly serious at this stage. The Bible views the fall of Adam and Eve as a great evil, in no way positive. It brought a curse on the entire human race that negatively affected the rest of creation as well. Physical death or mortality, a part of that curse, could only be overcome by the death of Christ on the cross (see Rom. 1:18–32). On these matters, Christianity and Mormonism are clearly opposed to each other.

MORMONISM AND SALVATION

It is commonplace today for Mormon missionaries and advocates of the Mormon faith to speak of Jesus Christ as their Savior and Lord. They also often mention having a personal relationship with him. This trend has not always been the case.

Using the same term but with a different meaning is an old ploy. The apostle Paul warned the first-century church at Corinth to be careful when people used the name of Jesus Christ carelessly. "For if he who comes preaches another Jesus whom we have not preached . . . or a different gospel which you have not accepted— you may well put up with it!" (2 Cor. 11:4). While Christ may be discussed by someone, it does not mean that he or she is speaking of the same Jesus referred to by Bible-based Christians.

We must always remember that Mormonism has a different Jesus. He is one of many gods in the Mormon pantheon. He is the firstborn spirit child of Elohim, having been sired by the Mormon God both in the premortal spirit state, as well as with Mary when he came to earth.

Not only does Mormonism teach a different *person* of Christ, it also teaches a different *work* or *atonement* of Christ. The Mormon gospel outline contains these six elements:

1. God's righteousness demands the punishment of sin.[18]

2. The Mormon Jesus was the "only begotten" or sired Son of God by Mary and is the only being capable of making an atonement.

3. Jesus made an "infinite and eternal" atonement for all the sins of the children of God—beginning in Gethsemane and ending at the resurrection.[19]

4. Jesus' atonement "affects worlds without number" and will save all of God's children, except the "sons of perdition."[20]

5. Christ's atonement "secured a resurrection for all the children of God."[21]

6. All who do the "full will of God" will receive the "full benefit" of the atonement.[22]

While appearing, at least superficially, to be evangelical, a closer look at the Mormon doctrine of "general or unconditional salvation" will help clarify the unbiblical positions of Mormonism. General salvation is the doctrine that Christ's death on the cross secured a measure of salvation for everyone. It is the belief that through Jesus all people will be raised to experience a better existence: "[B]ecause of Jesus Christ came the resurrection of man. And because of the redemption of man which came by Jesus Christ, they are brought back into the presence of the Lord; yea, this is wherein all men are redeemed" (Mormon 9:12–13).

Mormon theologian and apostle Bruce McConkie put it succinctly: "Unconditional or general salvation, that which comes by grace alone without obedience to gospel law, consists in the mere fact of being resurrected."[23]

Without the death of Christ there would have been no resurrection from the dead. With it, all people may experience a blissful eternity in one of three levels of heaven—celestial, terrestrial, or telestial. Mormonism also claims that Christ's death brought salvation to an "infinite number of earths,"[24] a notion that fits the Mormon view that an infinite number of worlds exist.

This Mormon doctrine of salvation contradicts the Bible at several key points. First, it is clear that the Resurrection, according to the Bible, is both for the just and the unjust (Acts 24:15). It will be a resurrection to eternal glory for the saved and to a life of punishment without God for those outside of Christ.[25]

Second, for a person to be saved, the Bible is very clear that one must put faith in Christ for that salvation. Scripture plainly states that the entire human race is under the condemnation of sin. To have eternal life at any level of reward, one must have a personal and saving relationship with Jesus Christ (Rom. 3:21–30; Gal. 3:6–4:7). He who has the Son, Scripture says, has eternal life. He who does not have the Son does not have life but the wrath of God abides on him (John 3:36; 1 John 5:12). Belief in Christ and faith in Christ are like breathing for the believer. Without faith it is impossible to please God—so declares the Bible (Heb. 11:6).

Even with this clear truth revealed by Scripture, Mormonism has devised a system where belief is not necessary for salvation. Indeed, it also teaches that good works or suffering for sin must complement grace at every step.

Let's look closer at the Mormon concept of eternal life. Here we will continue to discover how distant Mormonism is from biblical teaching.

MORMONISM AND ETERNAL LIFE

The LDS Church teaches that salvation has been achieved by the work of Christ. It is awarded to three different classes of people at three different levels of eternal reward—the *telestial* (the lowest heaven) and the *terrestrial* (higher up the scale of blessing). The highest level of eternal reward is the *celestial* kingdom. For

Mormons, participation at the fullest form in this life, or in the life to come, fits a person for the ultimate blessing of the celestial kingdom.

Three Levels of Reward

The terrestrial kingdom is the second-highest heaven. It is reserved in the "post-mortal spirit world" for those "who rejected the gospel on earth but afterward received it in the spirit world. These are the honorable people on the earth who were blinded to the gospel (i.e., the laws and ordinances of the LDS Church) of Jesus Christ by the craftiness of men. These are also they who received the gospel and a testimony of Jesus but then were not valiant."[26] (The phrase regarding a testimony is a Mormon reference to the "burning of the bosom," which will be explained soon.) Most of the inhabitants of the terrestrial kingdom, it seems, are inactive or at least not fully faithful Mormons. They will benefit in that realm in four ways:

1. They will enjoy the presence of Jesus but not the Father.
2. They will minister to those in the lower or telestial kingdom.
3. They will exercise power, might, and dominion over the telestial kingdom.
4. They will be resurrected after those inheriting the celestial kingdom.[27]

It is important to note that the "goodness and righteousness" of these people enabled them to qualify for the terrestrial realm. Their good works were added to Christ's grace.

Who will inherit the telestial kingdom—the lowest of the three levels of heaven? It will be people who "profess to follow Christ—but willfully reject the gospel"—or, once again, Mormonism. Included with the rejecters of "the everlasting covenant" are "murderers, liars, sorcerers, adulterers and whoremongers."[28] It is not through faith in Christ that people at this level will be advanced to the next heavenly level, but rather they will "become clean through their suffering,"[29] referring to the trials endured by these souls in spirit prison prior to the general resurrection. Mormonism advocates, then, a form of purgatory. This level of salvation is achieved, not by grace, but by suffering and paying for one's sins in spirit prison.

Hell is a special category that is related to the highest level of the celestial kingdom. The celestial kingdom, the highest level of reward, has an amazing list of five blessings for those worthy Mormons who will achieve it:

1. They will experience the "fulness of joy."
2. They will have "eternal life with heavenly father and Jesus Christ."
3. They "will become gods."
4. They will have "their righteous family members with them" and "will be able to have spirit children also."
5. They will have "all power, glory, dominion and knowledge," or everything God and Jesus have.[30]

These last two "blessings" form the view that worthy Mormons progress to godhood in the celestial realm. Entrants to the celestial kingdom eventually receive attributes that, according to the Bible, can only belong to one being in the universe, God himself. It is actually impossible for more than one being to have "all" of anything, especially attributes that can belong only to God. Nonetheless, Mormonism claims that most people who enter the celestial realm will finally possess divine attributes.

How does a Mormon qualify for godhood? At this point the Mormon Church clearly sets the standards for celestial glory. While some of the details are not clear, there are, it seems, at least twelve steps to godhood.

Step 1: Have faith in Christ. But the question then comes, "Which Christ?" For the Mormon it is the Christ who was literally the Son of God in both the premortal spirit realm and in the earthly realm through the heavenly Father's sexual union with Mary. The Bible declares that it is only through faith in Jesus Christ, the Second Person of the Christian Trinity, that brings full salvation. In the Mormon system, the Jesus is different and faith is only the first step.

Step 2: Be repentant. Repentance for the Mormon is not just turning from sin to Christ but includes spending "the balance of your lives trying to live the commandments of the Lord so he can eventually pardon you."[31] Repentance becomes, therefore, a work to be performed with the hope that one might be forgiven.

Step 3: Be baptized by the LDS Church. The LDS Church claims to be the only true church. It recognizes only baptism performed by "a duly commissioned servant or representative of the savior" as legitimate.[32] The "servant" must be an Aaronic priesthood holder, and then baptism becomes "the gateway through which we enter the celestial kingdom."[33]

Step 4: Accept the laying on of hands by a member of the Melchizedek Priesthood to receive the Holy Ghost. This rite is the reason that Mormons often refer to themselves as being born again through the Holy Ghost. To receive the Holy Ghost, one must be baptized by a member of the Melchizedek Priesthood since "the authority to bestow the Holy Ghost belongs to the Melchizedek Priesthood, and them alone."[34]

Step 5: Males are ordained into the Melchizedek Priesthood. This rite is performed when a Mormon male is prayed for by an already active member of the order. The rite "is designed to enable men to gain exaltation in the highest heaven."[35]

Step 6: Receive temple endowments. The rites and rituals of sealing, anointing, and marriage performed in Mormon temples are occasions when the recipients "are taught the things that must be done . . . in order to gain exaltation."[36]

Step 7: Participate in celestial marriage. This ritual is especially important for Mormons so that when they become gods they may have spouses with whom to procreate spirit children.[37]

Step 8: Observe the word of wisdom. The "word of wisdom" dictates the Mormon dietary code, including the phrase that advises Mormons against "strong" and "hot drinks," which are deemed off-limits in order that Mormons may experience "not only prolonged life, but life eternal."[38]

Step 9: Sustain the prophet. To reject the message of the prophet and president of the Mormon Church is tantamount to rejecting "the Lord himself" and becoming unworthy of the celestial kingdom.[39]

Step 10: Tithe. "One tenth of the interest or increase of each member of the church is payable into the . . . funds of the church each year." The tithe "is essential to the attainment of those great blessings which the Lord has in store for his . . . saints." *Doctrine and Covenants* is even more explicit: "He that is tithed shall not be burned at his [Jesus'] coming."[40] These statements teach that paying a tithe is essential to receiving the celestial blessing and avoiding judgment by Christ.

Step 11: Attend sacrament meetings. These occasions are the weekly gatherings on Sundays for Mormons. The meetings are for the purpose of renewing covenant vows and ensuring that members "have the Lord's spirit . . . with us" and thereby gain" a remission of our sins."[41]

Step 12: Obey the church. Continued participation in the church is essential for conditional salvation. Hell, in fact, is reserved for apostates who leave the church. (See fig. 6.2.)

In conclusion, no one can ever be certain of achieving this conditional understanding of salvation. It is a state of blessing that will only be realized in the world to come. At some stage, however, even for the Mormon, grace does form part of the equation. According to the *Book of Mormon,* "it is by grace that we are saved after all that we can do" (2 Nephi 25:23). Grace for the Mormon is their last hope. It is merely frosting on the cake. For Christians, on the other hand, grace is their only hope; it is both cake and icing: "For by grace you have been saved through faith" (Eph. 2:8). When one adds good works or Mormon attributes to grace, grace changes. It is no longer trust only in God's forgiveness through Christ; it becomes confidence in one's good or religious works as well. When oxygen stands alone, it is life-giving. When even one part of carbon is added to it, though, it becomes carbon monoxide, which deprives one of life-giving oxygen. The same principle is true of grace—it only gives eternal life when it stands alone.

Exaltation and Baptism for the Dead

There is one way in which a person might be able to achieve the celestial kingdom along with exaltation to godhood without becoming a temple-worthy Mormon in this life. A person, once

FROM CREATION TO EXALTATION

Celestial Kingdom
- Temple-worthy Mormons achieve godhood
- Children who die in infancy
- Those who have never heard of Mormonism and have proxy baptism and marriage may achieve the celestial kingdom

Terrestrial Kingdom
- Reserved for good and honorable people
- Inactive Mormons are assigned here

Telestial Kingdom
- Adulterers, liars, and thieves
- Rejectors of Mormonism
- Sins are paid for in spirit prison
- Suffering during millennium

Hell and Outer Darkness
- Apostates from the Church of Jesus Christ of Latter-day Saints
- Those who reject Mormonism in spirit prison are also condemned to this place
- The devil and the fallen spirits of the pre-mortal estate

PARADISE
(Baptized Mormons)

SPIRIT PRISON
Elevation possible by proxy baptism

Premortal Existence

1/3 A person may prove to be valiant for Jesus and this increases their chances to achieve the celestial kingdom.

1/3 Unfaithful spirits rebel with Satan and are condemned to be demons. They will be sent to the outer darkness.

1/3 One third of the spirits are not supportive of Jesus and are cursed with dark skin in their mortal life. They will be less receptive to the gospel.

On Earth people either accept Mormonism or are relegated to a lower realm

Figure 6.2

90

dead, could be baptized by proxy in a Mormon temple. The dead person, according to LDS doctrine, would have to accept the Mormon baptism in spirit prison and then be elevated to paradise. In the resurrection and judgment to follow, if he still holds to his Mormon faith, he could then be accepted into the celestial kingdom.

According to Mormonism, millions of people, long since dead, have been redeemed in this way. LDS teaching states, "The Lord has commanded that vicarious baptisms be performed to enable those who receive the gospel in the spirit world to enter his kingdom."[42]

While the Mormon Church often cites 1 Corinthians 15:29, "Why then are they baptized for the dead?" as justification of this practice, nowhere does the Bible instruct the church to baptize by proxy. It is possible that baptism was done at Corinth, perhaps for people who believed but had no chance to experience believers' baptism before their deaths. It certainly is clear that the promise of obtaining a higher level of heaven by proxy baptism is never endorsed by Scripture.

How many people would qualify for proxy baptism in Mormon practice? As many as could be traced through genealogical study and who were never exposed to the teachings of Mormonism. This belief is the reason for the Mormon Church's expansive and extensive genealogical records.

The fact that the deceased Adolf Hitler was baptized, ordained to the priesthood, and married to Eva Braun in a Mormon temple ceremony demonstrates that faith and repentance in this life is not an essential feature of celestial glory or any level of Mormon salvation.[43]

Hell Perdition or Outer Darkness

According to Mormonism, hell is for the apostates, the rebels who leave the LDS Church after receiving a testimony by the Holy Ghost that Mormonism is true. "Those who in mortality have known the power of God, have been made partakers of it . . . then later denied the truth . . . will have no forgiveness and will be the sons of perdition . . . [who will] suffer the wrath of God and partake of the second death."[44] It appears then that it is more dangerous to be a member of the Mormon Church than not. Only if one joins the church, believing its claims, can one be in danger of God's wrath and eternal separation from him.

Along with apostates from the LDS Church, the "premortal spirits who sided with Satan in his rebellion against God will also merit hell."[45]

DEBT VERSUS NO DEBT

While on the surface the Mormon doctrine of salvation appears to have a lot in common with biblical Christianity, a closer study demonstrates large differences. What is the basis of salvation for the Mormon? Works and obedience to the LDS Church! In the Mormon missionary book *Gospel Principles,* a story is told of a man who owes a great debt. He is unable to pay it. A friend, however, intervenes and offers to pay the creditor and save the friend from prison. Then the friend says to the debtor, "If I pay your debt, will you accept me as your creditor?"

"Oh yes, yes," cried the debtor. "You saved me from prison and show [sic] mercy to me."

"Then," said the benefactor, "you will pay the debt to me and I will set the terms. It will not be easy, but it will be possible. I will provide a way. You need not go to prison."[46]

The debt still had to be paid! And for the Mormon, there is a debt of service to be paid to the Church of Jesus Christ of Latter-day Saints.

For the Bible-based Christian, Jesus has paid all our debts. In fact, Jesus told a parable about forgiven debts in Matthew 18:21–35. A king forgave his servants their debts to him. One ungrateful servant, however, turned afterward and demanded payment from a colleague for a very small amount. Unable to pay, the second servant was thrown into prison. Jesus used this story to illustrate the point that we should forgive one another just as God has completely forgiven us through Christ.

The biblical gospel of Jesus Christ is that no debt remains to be paid. Jesus suffered sufficiently on the cross so that everyone who believes in him may be forgiven of all wrongs—past, present, and future. No works or human suffering ever need to be added to the work of Christ. His work is sufficient for us all.

There are at least eight key differences between Mormonism and biblical Christianity regarding the doctrine of salvation.

1. Mormonism teaches that Christ provides a form of salvation for all. Christianity teaches that only those who believe in the cross of Christ are saved.

2. Mormonism teaches that the highest form of salvation is available only to faithful Mormons. Christianity teaches that rewards are at God's discretion for all Christians.

3. Mormonism teaches that baptism for the dead provides an opportunity for all to receive the celestial blessing. Christianity teaches that life on earth provides the only opportunity to be saved.

4. Mormonism teaches that even if a person does not believe, he or she will be saved. Christianity teaches that faith in Christ saves.

5. Mormonism teaches that grace is effective after all that a person does. Christianity teaches that grace is the only grounds for God's forgiveness in Christ.

6. Mormonism teaches that the false Christ of Mormonism provides salvation. Christianity teaches that only the Christ of the Bible is sufficient for salvation.

7. Mormonism teaches that hell is reserved for the rebellious premortal spirits and apostates from the LDS Church. Christianity teaches that hell is for all sinners who remain unreconciled to God outside of Christ.

8. Mormonism teaches that worthy Mormons will become gods in the celestial kingdom due to their obedience. Christianity teaches that saved Christians will dwell in God's presence—Father, Son, and Holy Spirit. Christians will be like Christ in his moral qualities. Salvation is God's gift due to believers' faith in Christ.

WITNESSING POINTS

- Mormons redefine Jesus to interpret him as a "literal" Son of God in the premortal spirit state, as well as physically in this life.
- The word *gospel* for the Mormon means the laws and ordinances of Mormonism, not the good news of salvation through faith in Jesus Christ.
- Mormons believe that everyone—excluding apostates from the LDS Church—will have a better existence in the life to come, but no Mormon has assurance of God's ultimate blessings.
- Christians believe everyone has fallen short of God's holiness. Everyone in the human race is a sinner.
- Christians believe the truth that Jesus Christ died on the cross for all the sins of the world, not just for Adam's original sin.
- Christians believe that salvation is God's gift. It is not something that a person earns.

Chapter 7

REVEALING REVELATIONS

T he Bible is God's infallible and inerrant Word! Do you believe that?" Mary asked her Mormon friend.

"Of course I do!" Jane said. "Here's my Bible right here." She picked up a large, brown, leather-covered book on her coffee table and handed it to Mary. It read *Holy Bible.* "See, we believe and use the Bible like you do!"

"What translation is this?" Mary asked.

"It's the King James Version, of course," Jane said. "It's the official version of our church." She turned to the title page and pointed to the words "Authorized King James Version." Beneath the title was written, "Published by the Church of Jesus Christ of Latter-day Saints."

"I always thought your church didn't believe the Bible," Mary said apologetically. "I thought you had some other book. You know, the *Book of Mormon*."

"That's just what some people say to distort our church's beliefs," Jane said. "True, we also have the *Book of Mormon*, but it only complements the Bible; it doesn't contradict it. I'll give you a copy so you can read it for yourself."

"Thanks," Mary said, looking at the cover that read *Book of Mormon: Another Testament of Jesus Christ*. She opened it and scanned a page or two. "You know, it reads just like the Bible!"

"Of course it does," Jane said. "It's just like the Bible. It's just another testament of Jesus Christ."

The Church of Jesus Christ of Latter-day Saints regards the King James Version of the Bible as its official translation. They publish it and even distribute copies free to those requesting it. But is Jane correct in her claim that Mormons believe and use the Bible just like other Bible-believing Christian churches? Is she right about the *Book of Mormon* complementing the Bible and being just "another testament" of Christ? And if Mormons believe the Bible is augmented by the *Book of Mormon*, as the Word of God, are there other books they also consider inspired? Most important of all, what do the *Book of Mormon* and other Mormon writings teach? Are they truly compatible with historic Christian theology?

MORMONS AND THE BIBLE

Mormons use the Authorized King James Version (KJV), meaning the translation authorized by the English King James in 1611. To document their claims of belief in the Bible as the Word of God, they often point to the first clause in article eight of the LDS Church's thirteen *Articles of Faith* written by Joseph Smith Jr.: "We believe the Bible to be the word of God as far as it is translated correctly."

That statement would be hard for any Bible believer to dispute. But what exactly did Joseph Smith mean by it? Apparently, he did not regard the standard translations of his day, including the KJV, as "translated" correctly. According to Smith, and as still taught today by the LDS, all the existing biblical texts were corrupted and altered by what Mormons call the "Great Apostasy" of the post-apostolic church (see chaps. 3 and 8). They often claim many important passages of Scripture were removed by paganized ecclesiastical powers. "Wherefore, thou seest that after the book hath gone forth through the hands of the great and abominable church that there are many plain and precious things taken away from the book, which is the book of the Lamb of God" (1 Nephi 13:28).

Thus, they say all texts, by which modern translations were derived, are essentially flawed. The clear implication is that none are "translated correctly," since they are not transmitted correctly from the original manuscripts. Joseph Smith was reported to have stated, "From sundry revelations which had been received, it was apparent that many important points touching the salvation of men had been taken from the Bible or lost before it was compiled."[1]

Smith, in fact, claimed that God intended for him to publish an accurate and fully restored version of the Bible. Beginning in 1830, and until his death in 1844, Smith worked on his own "inspired version," or the "Joseph Smith Translation" (JST). He boldly claimed that, through a miraculous work of God, he was able to correct, add, or delete literally hundreds of words, phrases, or whole passages that were inaccurately written in standard versions of the Bible. He even deleted one entire book from his version, The Song of Songs (or Song of Solomon).

Today, though the KJV remains the official LDS version, the LDS Church still recognizes the JST as an inspired work. Herald House Publishing of the Reorganized Church of Jesus Christ of Latter Day Saints provides copies for sale in LDS bookstores, so it is widely circulated among Mormons. Also, recent LDS versions of the KJV have included footnotes and appendixes referencing or quoting Smith's alterations.

A CHRISTIAN RESPONSE

Despite repeated claims to the contrary, the LDS Church does not actually believe the Bible is accurate and can be trusted. They regard it, at the very best, as incomplete. At the worst, they think it has been tainted beyond reliability.

Christian scholars would respond that the Bible texts currently in existence are within 1 percent of complete textual accuracy. The claim that the Hebrew (Old Testament) and Greek (mostly New Testament) texts were seriously corrupted in the early centuries after Christ cannot be substantiated. In fact, the textual evidence for the reliability and completeness of both the Old and New Testaments has been confirmed by scholars from many sources. Many of the extant texts of the Old Testament, such as those discovered in the famous Dead Sea Scrolls, date to several centuries prior to Christ. Some New Testament texts now available date as early as the second century after Christ. The textual evidence for the biblical documents are the best attested of any ancient writings known.[2]

This is why Christians can confidently affirm that what the Bible says about itself is true: it is the authoritative Word of God and sufficient revelation for salvation, doctrine, and instruction. It was written by men inspired by the Holy Spirit and has been carefully preserved (see Deut. 4:1–2; Ps. 119:11, 89, 105, 140; Luke 21:33; Rom. 15:4; 2 Tim. 3:15–17; Heb. 1:1; 4:12; 1 Pet. 1:25; 2 Pet. 1:19–21).

On the other hand, Joseph Smith's revisions in his JST are without justification. His claims to having divine inspiration must be rejected since the Bible's indisputable textual evidence actually contradicts his revisions at nearly every point.

Also, the LDS Church's reliance solely on the KJV as its official translation is difficult to understand in light of the enormous advance in textual and linguistic studies since its seventeenth-century publication. The majority of biblical scholars today are respectful of the dignified style and spiritual impact of the KJV on the English-speaking world. However, they recognize that its textual base (the *Textus Receptus*) has been vastly surpassed in the last couple of centuries by discoveries of far more ancient manuscripts. Its linguistic style (Elizabethan English), while beautiful and dignified, is archaic and difficult for today's reader to comprehend.

The truth is, the Bible plays only a small part in the religion of Mormonism anyway. Most Mormons have a superficial understanding of the Bible; most know familiar Bible stories and some verses that are used as proof texts for LDS teachings. Little or no LDS theology is really derived from the Bible.

It is the other extrabiblical scriptures of the LDS, and the official statements of LDS prophets/presidents, that are the true sources of Mormon doctrine. The LDS Church's written scriptures, called the "Four Standard Works," include the KJV Bible, the *Book of Mormon: Another Testament of Jesus Christ*, *Doctrine and Covenants* (D&C), and the *Pearl of Great Price* (PGP). The LDS Church no longer publishes the D&C and PGP separately. In fact, all four works are now available under a thick, single-cover volume nicknamed the "Quad."

THE *BOOK OF MORMON*

The best known of the special LDS writings is the *Book of Mormon*. The novel story of Joseph Smith Jr.'s supposed discovery and translation of the golden plates was discussed somewhat in chapter 3. Here we will examine in more detail the creation, contents, credibility, and utilization of the *Book of Mormon* in the LDS system.

In chapter 1, we recounted how Elder Watson encouraged his potential converts, Joe and Sue, to read the *Book of Mormon* and pray about its validity. He pointed to a promise found in Moroni 10:4: "And when ye shall receive these things, I would exhort you that ye would ask God, the Eternal Father, in the name of Christ, if these things are not true; and if ye shall ask with a sincere heart, with real intent, having faith in Christ, he will manifest the truth of it unto you, by the power of the Holy Ghost."

Mormon missionaries and church members often give inquirers a free copy of the *Book of Mormon* and sometimes include in its inside cover a written testimony of their own assurance of its veracity. That assurance comes, so they believe, as a result of obedience to the above command in Moroni. Somehow, God impresses upon them that the stories and teachings of the *Book of Mormon* are historically true and spiritually nourishing. This inner subjective confirmation is the first step in the process of conversion for most people entering the LDS Church. It may, indeed, be the *Book of Mormon's* most important function.

The questions remain, nonetheless: Is the *Book of Mormon* what the LDS claim it is? Is it true? And most important, what does it teach? We will examine each of these issues.

THE *BOOK OF MORMON* STORY

The *Book of Mormon* claims to be a historical record of several groups of people who lived first in ancient Palestine and later in the Western Hemisphere. It begins about the year 600 B.C. in Jerusalem where a Hebrew prophet named Lehi received a revelation from God ordering him, his wife, his four sons, and other Jews to flee Palestine to escape the coming captivity in Babylon. Lehi and his sons, under God's direction, built a ship, and, guided by divine revelation, sailed from the Red Sea across the Indian and Pacific Oceans until they made landfall somewhere in Central or South America.

Lehi's sons were named Laman, Lemuel, Sam, and Nephi. According to the *Book of Mormon*'s story, Laman and Lemuel rebelled against the authority of Lehi and even against God. For that reason they were given a curse, which was marked by dark skin: "And he had caused the cursing to come upon them, yea, even a sore cursing, because of their iniquity. For behold, they had hardened their hearts against him, that they had become like unto a flint; wherefore, as they were white, and exceedingly fair and delightsome, that they might not be enticing unto my people the Lord God did cause a skin of blackness to come upon them" (2 Nephi 5:21).

Thus, the descendants of Lehi divided into two nations, the righteous, light-skinned Nephites and the wicked, rebellious, dark-skinned Lamanites. Most of the *Book of Mormon*'s fifteen books tell of the conflicts between the Nephites and Lamanites over the course of a thousand years, from about 600 B.C. until just after A.D. 400.

The most significant single event described in the volume is found in the books of 3 and 4 Nephi. According to those texts, Jesus Christ himself visited the Americas in the days following his resurrection. "And it came to pass, as they understood they cast their eyes up again toward heaven; and behold, they saw a Man descending out of heaven; and he was clothed in a white robe; and he came down and stood in the midst of them; and the eyes of the whole multitude were turned upon him, and they durst not open their mouths, even one to another, and wist not what it meant, for they thought it was an angel that had appeared unto them. And it came to pass that he stretched forth his hand and spake unto the people, saying: Behold, I am Jesus Christ, whom the prophets testified shall come into the world" (3 Nephi 11:8–10).

For three days Jesus ministered among the Nephites and Lamanites. He established a church among them complete with twelve apostles and the holy priesthoods. He taught them great ethical and spiritual truths, and initiated the ordinances of baptism and the Lord's Supper. Much of what he said was very similar to what he had taught during his life in Palestine. The *Book of Mormon* claims that these people were the "other sheep" about which Jesus had hinted in his earlier ministry (John 10:16).

Eventually, the church Jesus founded in the New World fell into divisions and apostasy, just as did the one in the Old World. Wars and conflicts continued between the Nephites and Lamanites until, finally, about the year A.D. 400, a great battle took place near a hill called Cumorah (Mormon 6). In that battle, all but 24 Nephites, out of an army of more than 230,000, were killed. Most Mormons today believe that the hill of Cumorah is near the current location of Palmyra, New York, not far south of Lake Ontario.

The last great Nephite leader was a general named Mormon who survived the war. In the days before his death, he collected and edited a set of golden plates upon which had been engraved, in a language called "reformed Egyptian" (Mormon 9:32), the history and wisdom of the Nephite and Lamanite peoples. Mormon passed the golden plates to his son Moroni, who added a concluding record about his father, the fate of the last Nephites, and himself. The *Book of Mormon's* other people, the Lamanites, survived and are ancestors to the Native American population.

Moroni added one other book to the collection. This book, which Moroni edited from twenty-four plates into a short volume, told a totally different tale than those found in other sections of the *Book of Mormon*. It described the adventures of a group of people who had come to America about the time of the tower of Babel—more than four thousand years ago. The followers of a man named Jared left the Near East about 2200 B.C. in eight barges illuminated by divinely-powered, glowing rocks. For 344 days the Jaredites drifted across the ocean until they arrived on the eastern shore of Central America.

The Jaredites grew in number and spread their culture throughout the Americas for several centuries until they finally died out. None remained when Lehi and his party landed in the sixth century B.C. However, the Jaredites' written record was uncovered by a Nephite King named Limhi about 121 B.C. The later Nephites added this "Book of Ether" to the collection of records that were edited by Mormon, hidden by Moroni, and later, in Joseph Smith's time, became the *Book of Mormon*.

JOSEPH SMITH AND
THE *BOOK OF MORMON*

According to the official LDS Church, as canonized in the *Pearl of Great Price* ("Joseph Smith—History"), the golden plates remained buried until 1823. That year, Joseph Smith, who had been called by God in 1820 to restore true Christianity to the earth, had a vision of an angel named Moroni. This angel Moroni was the same person who had buried the plates twelve hundred years earlier. He now appeared in a resurrected angelic form. He directed Smith to the exact location where the plates were buried. "Convenient to the village of Manchester, Ontario County, New York, stands a hill of considerable size, and the most elevated of any in the neighborhood. On the west side of this hill, not far from the top, under a stone of considerable size, lay the plates, deposited in a stone box."[3]

Smith was not allowed to take possession of the plates until September 22, 1827. On that date he took the golden plates, a miraculous instrument called the Urim and Thummim, and a breastplate. He began the tedious work of divinely inspired translation late that year.

Smith's wife, Emma, acted as his first recorder while they resided at her parent's home in Harmony, Pennsylvania. According to the descriptions by Emma and later scribes, Joseph would miraculously discern the writings on the plates while sitting behind a curtain. He read aloud the words as he deciphered them, and the scribes recorded them. Others who served in that function included Martin Harris, David Whitmer, and Oliver Cowdery, who apparently recorded the greatest portion.

Early in the process, Smith faced a crisis. Martin Harris was a Palmyra farmer who helped finance the project. His wife protested that Harris was spending too much time and money on Smith and demanded to see evidence that it was worthwhile. Smith reluctantly turned over to Harris 116 pages of manuscript they had completed to that point. Smith feared for their safety since they were the only copies he possessed.

His concerns proved warranted, for shortly thereafter, Harris reported back tearfully that the manuscript had inexplicably vanished. It was never recovered, so Smith was forced to translate again the section that was lost. However, his second version lacked much of the detail of the first. Smith maintained it was a more "spiritual" work. He was probably afraid that if the original was found it would demonstrate his translation's fallibility since it did not exactly match the second attempt.

Most LDS descriptions of the translation process say Smith utilized the Urim and Thummim as the instruments for translation. However, documented testimonies from several of those involved in the process, including Emma Smith and David Whitmer, described the process differently. Years later they stated that Smith actually used a small magic rock called a "seer stone" to comprehend the words on the plates and transcribe them into English. Smith found the stone years earlier while digging a well. He claimed it possessed occult divining properties for finding buried treasure (see chap. 3).

The *Book of Mormon* was finally completed and published in 1830. Five thousand copies of the original edition were produced by Egbert B. Grandin, a newspaper publisher in Palmyra. Smith included in his first edition two written testimonies of eleven men, all who claimed to have seen and touched the golden plates, along with his own description of the events surrounding the discovery and translation. Smith asserted that the original plates were returned to Moroni who took them to heaven.

In the nearly 170 years since the original edition, the *Book of Mormon* has undergone numerous revisions. Jerald and Sandra Tanner have documented nearly four thousand changes since the first edition, including some significant textual alterations.[4] Nonetheless, the *Book of Mormon* remains the best known extrabiblical LDS scripture. It has been translated from the English edition into more than sixty languages and is the focal point of Mormon missions and study.

EXAMINING THE *BOOK OF MORMON*

The official position of the LDS Church and the belief of most of its members is that the *Book of Mormon* is a divinely inspired and historically accurate ancient book given to Joseph Smith who translated it miraculously "by the gift and power of God." Many compelling facts, however, as documented by dozens of both LDS and non-LDS researchers, have cast grave doubts on the claims of Smith and the veracity of the *Book of Mormon*.

Historical Problems

The LDS Church says the *Book of Mormon* is an actual historical record of ancient civilizations located on the American continents. Mormons are hard put to explain, however, why no external archaeological record of any of the *Book of Mormon* people groups has ever been found. Decades of massive archaeological research have uncovered evidence of many great, pre-Columbian, Native American civilizations throughout South, Central, and North America. Unfortunately for LDS believers, nothing of substance has ever been found to confirm even one significant event recorded in the *Book of Mormon*. When it comes to the Bible, though, Near Eastern archaeological study has verified its credibility by uncovering many facts corroborating peoples, places, and events recorded in Scripture. No such confirmation can be found among New

World sites to corroborate claims of the *Book of Mormon*. Consider this list of eight nondiscoveries concerning the *Book of Mormon*:

1. No *Book of Mormon* cities have been found.
2. No *Book of Mormon* names have been found in New World inscriptions.
3. No genuine inscriptions have been found in Hebrew.
4. No genuine inscriptions have been found in Egyptian or anything similar to Egyptian, which could correspond to Joseph Smith's "reformed Egyptian."
5. No ancient copies of the *Book of Mormon* scriptures have been found.
6. No ancient inscriptions of any kind indicate that the ancient inhabitants held Hebrew or Christian beliefs. Instead, the beliefs of New World natives are pagan.
7. No mention of any people, nations, or places mentioned in the *Book of Mormon* have been found.
8. No artifacts of any kind that demonstrate the truth of the *Book of Mormon* have been found.[5]

Some LDS researchers have tried at various times to tie New World archaeological discoveries to the *Book of Mormon's* claims. To their chagrin, however, the Smithsonian Institution's National Museum of Natural History has provided a written statement denying the *Book of Mormon's* archaeological validity for inquirers for years.[6]

Another significant historical problem concerns the LDS Church's claim that Native Americans are descendants of pre-exilic Jews who migrated to America approximately twenty-six hundred years ago. This assertion contradicts every known anthropological study of Native American populations. The almost universally accepted view is that Native Americans are not descendants of Middle Eastern Jews, but of various Asian populations who migrated from Siberia across a now-submerged land bridge into Alaska and south into the Americas. Some theories place the earliest migrations as far back as thirty thousand to fifty thousand years ago.

Other historical problems involve anachronisms found throughout the *Book of Mormon*, such as reports of metals and weapons never known in pre-Columbian times. Biological and zoological anomalies also appear. Horses, cattle, elephants, and other animals are described in detail despite the undeniable facts that they were unknown in the Western Hemisphere until after Europeans arrived more than a thousand years after the closing events of the *Book of Mormon*.

All these facts cast a great shadow of doubt on the truth of the *Book of Mormon*. What should we make of this? How reliable could we say the Bible is if there were absolutely no external support for any of the events, persons, places, or things it describes? Would we defend its veracity if we found numerous anachronisms, geographical errors, or biological inaccuracies in its passages? But the Bible has stood the test of rigorous objective scrutiny. Such cannot be said for the *Book of Mormon*.

Problems with Joseph Smith's Claims

The *Book of Mormon* stands or falls on the truthfulness of Joseph Smith's claims about its discovery and translation. Several key facts, however, call into question Smith's account of what happened.

For one, though Smith talked about the angel Moroni's visit of 1823 and the golden plates as early as 1827, he did not write the official version until 1838, fourteen years afterward. More important, other descriptions of the events have been found that vary considerably in their details from those in the official version.[7]

Also troubling is the evidence tying Smith to various occult practices. Until the late 1960s, Mormon apologists denied Smith used a seer stone, an object employed in some occultic practices. But the fact could no longer be denied. A Bainbridge, New York, court record was found documenting Smith's 1826 arrest on a charge of being a disorderly person as a "glass looker"—a reference to his using a seer stone.

One cannot help but question the character of Joseph Smith based on other known details of his life. For example, Smith was later charged with such crimes as bank fraud and treason. He also is known to have engaged in polygamy as early as 1835.

Alternative Theories of Origin

Skeptical researchers have offered a number of possible theories as to the origin of the *Book of Mormon* as alternatives to Joseph Smith's official version. One theory that has received much discussion is sometimes called the Solomon Spaulding Theory, based on collected affidavits and materials by Charles Shook in his book, *True Origin of the Book of Mormon*, published in 1914. The theory suggests that one of Smith's close associates, Sidney Rigdon, stole the manuscript of a novel written by a Pennsylvania minister named Solomon Spaulding. The novel supposedly described the origin of the American Indians and formed the basis of what Rigdon, Smith, and Oliver Cowdery later wrote as the *Book of Mormon*. Though the theory remains passable, it has never been proven.[8]

Another compelling theory is that Smith borrowed ideas from several previous books written in the early 1800s. One particular work by Ethan Smith, *View of Hebrews,* which was published in 1823, has numerous parallels to the *Book of Mormon*. It was published in Poultney, Vermont, and was probably available to Joseph Smith and his associates. Among the similarities are the following thirteen points:

- Both books set forth the Hebrew origin of the American Indian.
- Both books talk of an ancient book hidden and buried in the ground.
- Both speak of prophets and seers.
- Both mention the Urim and Thummim and a breastplate.
- Both speak of ancient Egyptian inscriptions.
- Both talk of a civilized and barbaric element in the population.
- Both have references to the destruction of Jerusalem.
- Both talk of the gathering of Israel "in the last days."
- Both quote extensively from Isaiah.
- Both speak of a great Gentile nation rising up in America in the last days to save Israel.

- Both speak of the practice of polygamy among the early people.
- Both speak of widespread ancient civilizations on the American continent.
- Both speak of an appearance of a white god on the American continent.[9]

Fawn Brodie wrote what many consider the best biography of Joseph Smith, *No Man Knows My History*. She thought that Smith himself was the primary source of the *Book of Mormon*. She considered him a brilliant young man who was more than capable of drawing together various sources and concocting the fictional stories in the book. Researcher Harry L. Ropp tended to agree: "Joseph Smith could have used his own natural genius and both the Spaulding manuscript and *View of Hebrews*, as well as other materials, to produce the *Book of Mormon*."[10]

Two other obvious sources of information for the *Book of Mormon* were the KJV Bible and the KJV Apocrypha. Several hundred biblical and apocryphal phrases and verses and names are used in the *Book of Mormon*. Also, many story lines are parallel to those found in biblical and apocryphal stories, with names and places altered to fit the *Book of Mormon* settings. Many direct usages of biblical verses and terms are found almost verbatim in the *Book of Mormon*.

Some of the biblical terms in the *Book of Mormon* occur completely out of time with their biblical usage. One example of such an anachronism is in Alma 36. A character named Alma tells his son Helaman of his conversion by an angel and his previous life persecuting "the church of God" (Alma 36:6, 9). Later he cries out, "O Jesus, thou Son of God, have mercy on me, who am in the gall of bitterness" (Alma 36:18). This event, recorded in the *Book of Mormon*, supposedly took place sometime before the year 73 B.C., seven decades before Jesus was even born and nearly a century before "the church of God" was established. Neither the New Testament name *Jesus* (an English transliteration of the Greek) nor the New Testament term *church* (an English translation for the Greek word *ecclesia*) occur in the Old Testament, or even in the intertestamental Apocrypha. It seems odd, at best, that Alma—who was totally unfamiliar with Greek, was supposedly a descendant of Hebrews who left the Middle East five hundred years earlier, and lived nearly a century before Christ and half a world away—would have used those terms.

For other examples, compare Mosiah 26:27 (dated 120–100 B.C.) with Matthew 24:41; 1 Nephi 22:25 (dated 588–570 B.C.) with John 10:16; and Enos 27 (dated 544–521 B.C.) wih John 14:2.

Theological Problems

Joseph Smith once made the statement, "I told the brethren that the *Book of Mormon* was the most correct of any book on earth, and the keystone of our religion, and a man would get nearer to God by abiding by its precepts than any other book."[11] His statement implies that the *Book of Mormon* contains the full essence of Mormon theology. The truth is, however, many LDS doctrinal beliefs are not derived from that source. In fact, much of the theology reflected in the *Book of Mormon* flatly contradicts standard LDS teachings.

For example, the book of Alma records a frank conversation between two Nephites named Amulek and Zeezrom: "And Zeezrom said unto him: 'Thou sayest there is a true and living God?' And Amulek said: 'Yea, there is a true and living God.' Now Zeezrom said: 'Is there more than one God?' And he answered, 'No'" (Alma 11:26–29). A short time later their conversation continues: "Now Zeezrom saith again unto him: 'Is the Son of God the very Eternal Father?' And Amulek said unto him: 'Yea, he is the very Eternal Father of Heaven and of earth, and all things which in them are; he is the beginning and the end, the first and the last'" (Alma 11:38–39). Amulek's monotheistic (and Trinitarian) assertions that there is only one God and that the Son is the same as the Father, as told to him by an angel, are clear contradictions of Mormon doctrine that the heavenly Father, his Son Jesus Christ, and the Holy Ghost are three separate and distinct gods. It also conflicts with traditional LDS teachings that there are many other gods and that righteous people may attain godhood in the celestial kingdom (see chaps. 4 and 6).

So, if the *Book of Mormon* and, obviously, the Bible are not the sources of LDS doctrine, what is? The answer to that question leads us to the other official "standard works" of the Church of Jesus Christ of Latter-day Saints. It is in these other "modern revelations" and "ancient scriptures" that most of the unique and unorthodox aspects of Mormonism have their origin.

THE *DOCTRINE AND COVENANTS*

In 1833 Joseph Smith published another book he titled *The Book of Commandments*. It contained sixty-five statements that he claimed were given to him by God as direct revelations between 1828 and 1831. In fact, Smith wrote in the first person, virtually quoting God's words as recorded in the Bible: "What I the Lord have spoke I have spoke, and I excuse not myself; and though the heaven and the earth pass away, my word shall not pass away, but shall all be fulfilled, whether by mine own voice or by the voice of my servants, it is the same."[12]

In 1835 Smith began to add new revelations to the book and changed its title to the current *Doctrine and Covenants.*

Until his death in 1844, Smith received dozens of communications from the Lord that were added to the book. Later, following his murder in Illinois, other LDS prophets, including Brigham Young, John Taylor, and Joseph Fielding Smith, added new sections. Today the *Doctrine and Covenants* contains 138 such revelations.

Two "Official Declarations" are also now included in the *Doctrine and Covenants.* The first, a statement by the fourth president, Wilford Woodruff, dated October 6, 1890, suspended the official LDS practice of plural marriage. The other was a statement from the First Presidency, then led by the twelfth president, Spencer W. Kimball, dated June 8, 1978, and sustained on September 30, 1978. It effectively overturned the long-standing LDS doctrine that prevented African American people from holding the LDS Church's priesthoods.

A number of key LDS doctrines are derived from *Doctrine and Covenants.* For example, section 89 contains the Mormon dietary code called the "word of wisdom." Mormons are advised to abstain from "wine or strong drink," tobacco, and "hot drinks," which they interpret to mean beverages containing caffeine, mainly coffee and tea.[13]

Section 124 commands the building of a temple for the practice of baptisms for the dead.[14] Section 128 contains further instructions and justification for the practice.

The LDS priesthoods are prescribed in Section 84: "And without the ordinances thereof, and the authority of the priesthood, the power of godliness is not manifest unto men in the flesh; for without this no man can see the face of God, even the Father, and live";[15] and in section 107: "There are, in the church, two priesthoods, namely the Melchizedek and Aaronic, including the Levitical priesthood."[16]

Perhaps the most controversial portion of *Doctrine and Covenants* is section 132. That revelation, supposedly received by Joseph Smith on July 12, 1843, but not made public until 1852, describes new terms and conditions to God's "everlasting covenant": "For behold, I reveal unto you a new and everlasting covenant; and if ye abide not that covenant, then ye are damned; for no one can reject this covenant and be permitted to enter my glory."[17] And what exactly did that "new and everlasting covenant" entail? "And again, as pertaining to the law of the priesthood—if any man espouse a virgin, and desire to espouse another, and the first give her consent, and if he spouse the second, and they are virgins, and have vowed to no other man, then is he justified; he cannot commit adultery for they are given unto him."[18]

This practice of plural marriage remained an officially endorsed LDS doctrine until the 1890 declaration of President Wilford Woodruff. Today polygamy is not sanctioned. Anyone who enters into it is derisively called a "fundamentalist" by other Mormons and is summarily excommunicated from the church. Nonetheless, the doctrine of "celestial marriage," as described in the revelation, remains in the canon of LDS scripture. Thus, the principle of plural marriage has not been negated, only postponed in Mormon practice to postmortem life in heaven or into the future millennial kingdom on earth.

THE *PEARL OF GREAT PRICE*

Most non-Mormons have heard of the *Book of Mormon*. Few, however, have ever heard of *Doctrine and Covenants*. Even less are familiar with the LDS' fourth written authority, the *Pearl of Great Price*. Published first in 1851 in England, it was not canonized as official LDS scripture until October of 1880. The *Pearl of Great Price* consists of five separate works supposedly written or translated by Joseph Smith between 1830 and 1842.

The first section, titled, "Selections from the Book of Moses," contains eight chapters and consists of extracts from the biblical Book of Genesis as found in Joseph Smith's translation. Most of it corresponds to the first six chapters of the KJV Book of Genesis. However, Smith added dozens of extra verses, some of which have significant theological importance for Mormonism. Consider the following examples.

A standard Mormon teaching is that all things, including human beings, had a preexistent spiritual life before they appeared on earth: "For I, the Lord God, created all things, of which I have spoken, spiritually, before they were naturally upon the face of the earth" (Moses 3:5).

Mormons also believe Satan's rebellion and fall was because he wanted to force all people to be redeemed instead of allowing them "free agency" to choose: "Wherefore, because that Satan rebelled against me, and sought to destroy the agency of man, which I, the Lord God, had given him, and also, that I should give unto him mine own power; by the power of mine Only Begotten, I caused that he should be cast down" (Moses 4:3). In other words, in Mormon theology, Satan's sin was that he wanted to deny the role of human freedom-of-choice in the salvation process so everyone would be saved, albeit blindly and by default. God, on the other hand, wanted to leave humans free to choose him or not. One of the bizarre notions this Mormon theology leaves us with is that Satan's plan would have led to the certain salvation of all, whereas God's plan will lead to the eternal loss of some souls. So Mormonism leaves us with the unbiblical and heretical conclusion that Satan is somehow more loving than God.

Mormons also regard the fall of Adam and Eve as a positive occurrence since they believe the Fall allowed humankind to become mortal and thus have the potential of "eternal progression": "And in that day Adam blessed God and was filled, and began to prophesy concerning all the families of the earth, saying: Blessed be the name of God, for because of my transgression my eyes are opened, and in this life I shall have joy, and again in the flesh I shall see God" (Moses 5:10). In no way does the Mormon auspicious outlook on the Fall align wih Christian theology.

We have already discussed the fallacy of Smith's view of the Bible and his presumptuous attempt to "correct" its texts "miraculously." Clearly we see that Smith's revision, here canonized in LDS scripture, included major theological distortions that fall outside the bounds of historic Christian orthodoxy.

The second section of the *Pearl of Great Price* is Joseph Smith's supposed translation of the Book of Abraham. This five-chapter document, according to the LDS Church, is an actual book written by the patriarch Abraham while he was in Egypt (Gen. 12:10–20).

The story of Smith's acquisition and translation of this book constitutes one of the most bizarre and embarrassing aspects of Mormon history. In 1835, while residing in Ohio, Smith purchased a set of ancient Egyptian artifacts from a peddler named Michael Chandler. According to Smith's own story, by a miraculous process he never explained, Smith was able to translate one piece of papyrus that he declared was written by Abraham. Smith translated the entire book over the course of several years and in 1842 published it as the Book of Abraham.

The papyrus used by Smith (now called the Joseph Smith Papyrus) was assumed to have been sold to a Chicago museum after his death and was believed destroyed in the Chicago fire of 1871. However, in 1967 it was discovered intact in the Metropolitan Museum of Art in New York City. It was quietly turned over to LDS Church officials, who reluctantly made it available for study by several skilled Egyptologists. The results of those studies demonstrated that it was actually a section of an ancient funerary text called "The Book of Breathings"—a part of the *Egyptian Book of the Dead*. This evidence casts serious doubts on the reliability of

Smith's miraculous translation. Researcher Harry L. Ropp concluded: "Joseph's translation in no way corresponds to the writing on the papyrus. From the 46 characters in the manuscript, Smith produced 1,125 English words, including over 65 proper names."[19]

Mormon apologists, in various ways, have tried to rescue the legitimacy of the Book of Abraham. Some have argued that the Joseph Smith Papyrus was not the same text Smith used in his translation. However, experts have proven conclusively that it was the same.[20] Regardless, the book remains unchanged in the LDS canon of scripture. To this date, the church has not adequately responded to the charge that Joseph Smith's translation was not only inaccurate but a complete fabrication.

Two possible reasons may explain the LDS Church's unwillingness to make this admission. One may be that if they acknowledge Smith's fallibility on this "inspired" work, it would naturally call into serious question his other supposed revelations, including the *Book of Mormon* and the *Doctrine and Covenants*.

The other possible reason Mormons are not willing to de-canonize the Book of Abraham is several of the LDS Church's most important doctrines are derived from its passages—for example, the idea that human beings had a preexistent life before birth. A primary source for that doctrine is found here: "Now the Lord had shown unto me, Abraham, the intelligences that were organized before the world was; and among all these there were many of the noble and great ones" (Abraham 3:22 [19–28]). Also, the LDS doctrine of a plurality of gods is clearly derived from chapters 4 and 5, which is Abraham's account of the creation story: "And then the Lord said: Let us go down. And they went down at the beginning, and they, that is the Gods, organized and formed the heavens and the earth" (Abraham 4:1).

The *Pearl of Great Price* also contains three other major sections. "Joseph Smith—Matthew" is Smith's "inspired" translation of Matthew 23:39–24:5. "Joseph Smith—History" is Smith's official version of his first vision of God and Jesus, his recovery of the golden plates, and his translation of the *Book of Mormon*. *Articles of*

Faith are thirteen concise statements written by Joseph Smith supposedly summarizing LDS beliefs for non-Mormon inquirers.

LDS SCRIPTURES

The "Four Standard Works" of the Church of Jesus Christ of Latter-day Saints are the KJV Bible, the *Book of Mormon*, the *Doctrine and Covenants*, and the *Pearl of Great Price*. They are regarded by Mormons as divinely inspired writings and, thus, are considered the Word of God. However, as we have shown, in each case the LDS Church claims for the authority and reliability of these extrabiblical works suffer serious question when examined objectively.

The LDS Church's claim of belief in the Bible's authority is insincere since Joseph Smith taught it was textually flawed and needed a divinely inspired revision, the "Joseph Smith Translation." The *Book of Mormon* lacks objective credibility. Smith's statements about its miraculous discovery and translation and its historical accuracy and internal consistency do not stand the test of careful investigation.

As important as the *Book of Mormon* seems to be in the Mormon system, most distinctive LDS doctrines are not derived from it and even contradict it. Most major LDS doctrines, in fact, are derived from the other two modern revelations, the *Doctrine and Covenants* and the *Pearl of Great Price*. Although Smith claimed these works were given by revelation from God, the contents reflect Smith's own evolving historical, theological, and moral perspectives.

Christians, therefore, reject the claims of the LDS Church to possess additional divinely inspired scripture. Christians affirm the traditional Protestant view that only the sixty-six books of the Old and New Testaments, as written in the autographs, are infallible and without error. We assert that God's Word—the Bible—is sufficient for salvation, doctrine, and practice. Furthermore, many credible translations now exist in English and most other languages that have solid textual credence. They are based on scores of ancient manuscripts that share an incredible degree of agreement.

WITNESSING POINTS

Christians engaging LDS members in witnessing encounters may want to focus some of the discussion on the issues of revelation and Scripture. If so, keep in mind the following points:

- Ask the Mormon why his church still regards the KJV as Scripture, yet traditionally has denied its textual authenticity. Explain why you find Joseph Smith's revised version to be unwarranted in light of the enormous evidence for the reliability of the Bible.

- Question Joseph Smith's accounts of the discovery and translation of the *Book of Mormon*. Point out, as well, why many researchers believe Smith may have relied on previously written sources as the basis for his book. Explain that there are many obvious historical and archeological problems contained in its pages. Ask the Mormon why it has undergone hundreds of revisions since 1830 or why it does not contain many of the most basic doctrinal tenets of Mormonism, if, as Joseph Smith stated, it is "the most correct book on earth."

- Ask why some revelations in the *Doctrine and Covenants* are no longer binding, such as section 132, which calls plural marriage an "everlasting covenant."

- Ask why the *Book of Abraham* is still considered LDS scripture even though Egyptologists have shown Smith's translation to be a hoax. The Mormon may respond, as some do, that maybe the papyrus they studied was not the same one Smith used. Point out that researchers have conclusively demonstrated that it is authentic.

- Be ready to respond when a Mormon "bears testimony" to the truthfulness of the *Book of Mormon* and to Joseph Smith as a prophet. The Mormon will often fall back on that totally subjective claim as a last resort when confronted with objective evidence. Remember, as Elder Watson told Joe and Sue, Mormons often describe a "burning in the chest or bosom" experience that, to them, confirms the Holy Ghost's attestation that Mormonism and its scriptures are true. Warn the Mormon against relying on feelings, since they may be manipulated or even counterfeited.

- Share your personal testimony of the Bible's trustworthiness, based on hundreds of years of archaeological and textual research (not your feelings). Also, testify to your faith in Jesus Christ, and focus on who he is and what he did (see chap. 5), not on your emotional or mystical feelings. Our faith and assurance is based on established facts of the gospel, not our experience.

Chapter 8
JESUS IS COMING AGAIN

aranatha—"Come again, Lord Jesus!"—has been the watchword of Christians for two millennia. Not only have believers confessed the death, burial, and resurrection of Christ but also the blessed hope of his reappearance. It is important to note that the last words the disciples heard from the angels at Christ's ascendance were the poignant reminder that he would also return in the same way he ascended, bodily and visibly.

Christians have believed the following seven things about Jesus' ascension and the end times:

1. Jesus bodily and visibly ascended into heaven.

2. Jesus will return the same way.
3. The Bible alone reveals the facts about Jesus' appearance.
4. When Jesus returns, he will introduce an earthly one-thousand-year (millennial) reign (some Christians interpret the millennium symbolically).
5. Christ will judge all people regarding their faith in him.
6. A general bodily resurrection of all people will occur.
7. People will be consigned in the final judgment according to their acceptance or rejection of God's salvation through the person and work of Christ.

While Christians sometimes have varied views regarding the millennium—whether it's literal or whether Christ will precede or follow the Christianization of the world—the basic outline above contains the essentials of biblical belief. The Apostles' Creed probably encapsulates the most concise statement of faith regarding the *parousia*, or coming of Christ: "On the third day he [Jesus] rose again from the dead, ascended to heaven and sits on the right hand of God the Father almighty. From there he will come to judge the living and the dead."

When a Christian glances at the Mormon view of the Second Coming, at first he or she might think it is the same as the one revealed in the Bible. After all, Mormonism speaks about the "signs of the end," "Christ's second coming," "resurrection and judgment," and the "millennium," as well as "final judgment." But just because Mormonism appears or sounds Christian does not mean it is. Appearances can be deceptive. Artificial fruit sitting on the dining room table may look, especially at a distance, to be the real thing. A closer examination, especially if one bites into the fruit, will reveal whether the red, gleaming apple is authentic or artificial.

Jesus taught the same concept. In Matthew's Gospel, Jesus exhorts his followers to examine trees by their fruit and not their appearance. He then comments that "many" in the day of judgment will call him "Lord" and even claim to have done great and good deeds in his name. Yet he will tell them, "I never knew you: depart from me" (Matt. 7:22).

So let's turn our focus to Mormon beliefs about last things, evaluating them through the lens of the Bible and orthodox Christian theology.

SIGNS LEADING TO THE END

Jesus spoke about the end times and the general indicators or signs that would occur just prior to his reappearance. Mark 13 and Matthew 24 both record the heart of his comments on this important subject. Jesus revealed that an increase in famines, earthquakes, plagues, and other awful events would precede his reappearance. He also declared that the gospel—the good news that Jesus is the Savior—would be proclaimed throughout the whole world. Today we see traumas and trials continuing to increase everywhere, and we're also seeing the gospel spreading to the ends of the earth.

Mormonism takes note of these developments but lists them somewhat differently and then defines them in a particularly LDS fashion. Why? Because Mormons are insistent that the Bible itself does not have the full and final truth about Christ's return. Rather, it is in the *Book of Mormon,* the *Doctrine and Covenants,* and the revelations given through the prophets and presidents of the Church that the last word about last things is revealed. One Mormon spokesman put it this way: "In frank and open terms, though we love the Bible, we get our doctrine from modern revelation. As curious as that principle may seem to some, it is nonetheless an important safeguard against doctrinal misdirection. The words of the biblical prophets can confirm, bear witness to, and illustrate the truths of modern revelation, but our knowledge of the gospel comes through what was revealed to Joseph Smith. Thus as we read the Bible, we interpret it in light of modern revelation."[1]

Biblically Similar

Chapters in the *Doctrine and Covenants,* as well as the *Book of Mormon,* are often cited in Mormon publications as containing definitive material on the end times. Notably the first set of signs has a resemblance to the Bible: "The love of men shall wax cold, and iniquity shall abound."[2] "All things shall be in commotion; and . . . fear shall come upon all people."[3] "We can expect earthquakes, disease, famines, great storms, lightnings, and thunder."[4] Often biblical passages like Matthew 24:6–7 are referred to. It is clear that Mormonism has copied and repeated the biblical signs.

Distinctly Mormon

Other signs of the end are distinctly Mormon, including the restoration of the gospel: "Prophets of old foretold the restoration of the gospel," and "in fulfillment of this prophecy, the angel Moroni and other heavenly visitors brought the gospel of Jesus Christ to Joseph Smith."[5] The production of a "coming forth of the *Book of Mormon*" is yet another element of Mormonism's twisting of end-times signs away from a Bible-only position. The LDS Church takes various texts out of context to maintain that passages like Ezekiel 37:16–20 (the stick of Ephraim) are referring to the *Book of Mormon:* "The *Book of Mormon* has been brought forth and is being taken to all the world."[6]

Even when it sounds like a particular sign could only refer to something biblical, Mormon writings add to the Bible to make the message false. Therefore, when it is noted that the gospel will be preached to all the world, the LDS Church claims that this is the gospel of Mormonism: "Ever since the restoration of the Church, missionaries have preached the gospel. The missionary effort has increased until now tens of thousands of missionaries preach in many countries of the world in many languages. Before the Second Coming, the Lord will provide a way to bring the truth to all nations."[7]

The same is true of the sign of the coming of Elijah, which is referenced in Malachi 4:5–6. Elijah will "restore the sealing powers so families could be sealed together. He would also inspire people to be concerned about their ancestors."[8] Sealing and "concern" about ancestors are referring to the Mormon temple ceremonies and baptism for the dead, both of which are unbiblical.

The last two signs often noted by LDS writings are clearly used only in Mormon "revelations" and occur in the same passages as the previously mentioned signs. The Lamanites are predicted to become a great people, and Missouri will be the site of the New Jerusalem. "Great numbers of Lamanites in North and South America and the South Pacific are now receiving the blessings of the gospel." Lamanites are a reference to Native Americans who are obviously not the Israelites the Mormons claim them to be. The building of the New Jerusalem refers to a "prophecy" Joseph Smith claimed was revealed to him: "A righteous city, a city of God, called the New Jerusalem . . . will be built in the state of Missouri in the United States."[9] No such city has been built in Missouri, for the main contingency of the LDS Church relocated to Utah, and there they constructed Salt Lake City. Joseph Smith's prophecy has yet to be fulfilled, but Mormons hope and expect that it shall be, as a sign of the end times.

Other Mormon signs of the end include the establishment of the United States, the creation of the U.S. Constitution, and the building of Mormon temples.[10] The first two of the above were already fulfilled at the time of the writing of Mormon scripture. They are therefore not prophecies. The third is self-fulfilling with the LDS Church actively involved in the construction of temples.

Above everything else, the continuing growth and numerical progress of the LDS Church are thought by Mormons to be the key signs leading to Christ's Second Coming. Mormons identify themselves as "the Zion of God," and they consider the unabated growth of the LDS Church inevitable: "When Zion descends from above, Zion will also ascend from beneath, and be prepared to associate with those from above. The people will be so perfected, ennobled, exalted and dignified in their feelings and so truly humble and most worthy, virtuous and intelligent that they will be fit, when caught up, to associate with that Zion that shall come down from God out of heaven."[11]

Within Mormonism is the conviction that not only are they a spiritual Zion but, as many Mormon thinkers confess, they are the actual historical Israel. Within their veins, they believe, flows the very blood of Israel itself. Even as late as 1994, Mormon thinkers have commented extensively about this idea: "We are literally of the seed of Abraham. Let's just drill it into ourselves. We are literally of the seed of Abraham. We are natural heirs according to the flesh. We are not adopted nor anything else."[12]

Such thinking is misguided and inaccurate. Some Jews may be in the LDS Church, but it is inconceivable that every Mormon could claim that Jewish blood actually is theirs. The theory, however, is used by Mormonism to claim a unique place and role for the LDS Church in the end times.

This view is an extension of the theory that Joseph Smith was directly descended from the biblical patriarch Joseph. Brigham Young stated, "Joseph Smith, junior, was foreordained to come through the loins of Abraham, Isaac, Jacob, Joseph, and so on down through the prophets and apostles; and thus he came forth in the last days to be a minister of salvation, and to hold the keys of the last dispensation of the fulness of times."[13] While Joseph Smith's family never claimed to be Jewish, nor could it even be substantiated, Mormon scriptures unilaterally say it is so. In fact, Smith concocted the idea himself and wrote it in *Doctrine and Covenants* 132:30–31.

Mormonism, once again, demonstrates that it is a religion based on the false claims of Joseph Smith. They are claims so outlandish that they have to be taken on blind faith—a faith that contradicts and reconstructs history.

JESUS' COMINGS AND DUTIES

Mormonism teaches that Jesus will come in four stages. First, Jesus will come secretly. He will appear, first of all, in Adam-ondi-Ahman, in Missouri. Adam-ondi-Ahman was prophesied by Joseph Smith in *Doctrine and Covenants* 116 to be the place of Christ's millennial reign, as well as the location of the garden of Eden.[14] There Jesus will apparently meet with Adam "the Ancient of Days, as father of the human family and God's chief agent." Adam will surrender to Jesus "his stewardship of the earth and 'keys to the kingdom.'"[15]

Second, Jesus will appear to those in the New Jerusalem, or Independence, Missouri. His purpose there will be to initiate "a secret appearance to selected members of his [LDS] Church. He will come in private to his prophet [that is, the president of the Mormon Church] and to the apostles then living." It seems that former presidents of the Church will be present as well because it says "those who have held keys and powers and authorities in all ages from Adam will also be present."[16] Part of Jesus' purpose will be to commission 144,000 Mormon high priests as missionaries to preach the gospel of the LDS Church to the rest of the world.[17]

Third, Jesus will reveal himself to the Jews in Jerusalem, who will be under siege as the course of the Battle Armageddon rages. They will be the "beleaguered sons of Judah, surrounded by hostile Gentile armies, who again threaten to overrun Jerusalem." Jesus will appear and set his feet on the Mount of Olives, "and it shall cleave in twain, and the earth shall tremble." It is believed that "the Lord Himself will then rout the Gentile armies, decimating their forces. Judah will be spared, no longer to be persecuted and scattered."[18]

In the final stage, Jesus will appear to the rest of the world. When the Mormon scriptures speak of this element of Christ's return, they sound very similar to the Bible. All nations will see Jesus "in the clouds of heaven, clothed with power and great glory; with all the holy angels; . . . And the nations of the earth shall mourn, and they that have laughed shall see their folly."[19]

The LDS teaching about the Second Coming centers around the Mormon Church. Christ's appearance will supposedly conform to the prophecies of Joseph Smith. He will, Mormons say, secretly appear to the church's president. He will commission their missionaries and fulfill their plans. All of these events are well outside the truth of the Bible and demonstrate again the outrageous teaching of the Mormon Church.

Having outlined the appearances of Christ, Mormonism then details the activity of Christ at the time of his appearing to the world. There are five essential duties involved. The first is, Jesus will cleanse the earth. According to Mormonism, "the wicked will be destroyed. All things that are corrupt will be burned, and the earth will be cleansed by fire."[20] These comments apparently make reference to the Mormon belief that the wicked will be purified in hell before they inherit the telestial kingdom. The earth will be cleansed but continue to be inhabited during the millennium.

Second, Jesus will judge his people. All of the nations will be judged and wicked people will be separated from the righteous.

Third, Jesus "will take his rightful place as king of heaven and earth." Even this element in the end-times scheme is affected by the priority given to the LDS Church. Jesus "will establish his government on the earth. The church will become part of that kingdom."[21] From statements like these we can deduce that the Mormon Church is synonymous, to Mormons, with the kingdom of God. They are one and the same. The kingdom of God equals the church, and the church equals the kingdom of God.

Fourth, Jesus will "complete the resurrection." The first segment will consist of those righteous people raised "to meet the Savior as he comes down from heaven." These are worthy Mormons who will "inherit the glory of the celestial kingdom."[22] After the millennium has begun, those who are worthy to receive the terrestrial kingdom will also rise.[23]

Fifth, Jesus will "usher in the millennium." The development and ministry of Mormons will play a very significant role, which we shall soon see. Next, however, let us look at more details about the resurrection and judgment.

THE RESURRECTION AND JUDGMENT OF THE DEAD

In the interim between death and resurrection, there is a place for spirits of dead people to dwell. For righteous Mormons that place is paradise.

The righteous dead "who have kept the commandments of the Lord [the teachings and ordinances of the LDS Church] are going to come forth" from paradise.[24] At that point their bodies will be reunited with their spirits. It will then be their assignment to serve with Christ during the millennium.

People who are worthy of terrestrial glory will also be raised from the spirit world—but in this case from spirit prison. Spirit prison is described in Mormon scripture as a place of suffering for "those who rejected the gospel" (that is, the laws and ordinances of Mormonism) and is an experience of torment for "both body and spirit."[25] Once both the inheritors of the celestial and terrestrial realms are raised, the first resurrection will be completed.

The second resurrection will actually occur after the millennium. This raising will have been preceded by the destruction "in the flesh" of those wicked "who are living at the time of the second coming of the Lord. . . . They, along with the wicked who are already dead" will have to wait until the end of the millennium. At that time "they can come forth from their graves." They will have been judged for not having "kept the commandments of the Lord." The prison house for spirits in the millennium will be a type of purgatory because "the unrighteous shall have to spend their time during the thousand years" repenting and cleansing "themselves through the things which they shall suffer."[26]

The Mormon concept of the resurrection, not unlike Christianity, comes in two stages. The first stage comes at the appearing of Christ for the righteous. The second will occur after the millennium for the wicked. But as we have seen, much of the judgment falling on the wicked is due to their failure to keep Mormon laws and commandments. A closer look at the millennium will demonstrate it to be a Mormon millennium and not a biblical one.

In the second resurrection, according to Mormon theology, all of "the remaining dead will rise to meet God. They will either inherit the telestial kingdom or be cast into outer darkness with Satan."[27] Apostates from the LDS Church are those who will be cast into hell or "outer darkness," to use the Mormon term.

THE MORMON MILLENNIUM

Millennium is simply the word for one thousand. Most Christians have believed, based on biblical revelation, that there will be a thousand-year reign of Christ on the earth. Mormons believe the same idea. Their Christ, however, is much different than the Christ of Christianity. So the Mormon millennium bears the marks of Joseph Smith. The unique ideas inserted into end-times theology, or eschatology, center on the LDS Church and its history, which have nothing to do with the Bible.

To see these differences clearly, we will focus on three key questions: Who will be present during the millennium? What will be done during the one thousand years of Mormon supremacy? What will conditions be like?

Who will be present? First of all, the Jesus of Mormonism will reign and rule on the earth. Mormon writers state that his headquarters will be shared between the "New Zion" of Independence, Missouri, and the other Zion of Jerusalem: "Our Lord and God shall govern his people from two world capitals, for out of Zion shall go forth the law, and the word of the Lord from Jerusalem" (Isa. 2:3). They explain the passage this way: "'And he shall utter his voice out of Zion'—meaning, Independence, Missouri—'and he shall speak from Jerusalem, and his voice shall be heard among all people.'"[28]

Apart from Jesus, "only righteous people will live on earth" and that means specifically those people who "will inherit either the terrestrial or celestial kingdom(s)."[29] These people will be "mortal beings." They will live to about one hundred years of age and then be translated into the "postmortal" spirit world without the bitter experience of death. Joseph Smith taught that "immortal beings will frequently visit the earth," while he and the "resurrected Saints" (or Mormons) will visit whenever they please or when necessary to help in the governing of the earth.[30]

While many of those dwelling on the earth during the millennial reign will be "nonmembers of the Church of Jesus Christ of Latter-day Saints," eventually "everyone will accept Jesus Christ as the Savior." This last phrase couched in Mormonese means that people will become LDS Church members having rejected "their false religions and ideas."[31]

What will be done? The millennium will be a period of "temple and missionary work"—the two great enterprises "for members of the Church."[32] The doctrines of Mormonism will not change. The conviction will be solidified that "baptism, the laying on of hands" by a priesthood authority, as well as "the temple ordinances—the endowment, temple marriages, and the sealing together of family units," will be conducted for both the living and the dead. Apparently everyone who has ever lived will be included in this work in thousands of Mormon temples built all over the world.

How will all of the information necessary for baptism for the dead be collected? "Resurrected beings will help us correct the mistakes we have made in doing research concerning our dead ancestors. They will also help us find the information we need to complete our records."[33] If the work in temples being done now is flawed and incomplete, then why not wait for the millennium and do it all properly then? But Mormons today press on with the task of finding relatives, even though much of their work may be incorrect and the rite of baptism of the dead is unbiblical.

Missionary work will be extended to "all people" so that everyone will embrace Mormonism—"the first principles of the gospel"—as it is expressed in Mormon words.

Another work during the Mormon millennium will be the collection of all of Mormon scripture. LDS teaching claims that much of divinely inspired scripture is still unrevealed or inaccessible to human beings. But during the one thousand years of Mormon supremacy, "we shall yet read the sealed portion of the Book of Mormon . . . the damning veil of unbelief shall be rent and we shall have a complete Book of Mormon. . . . We shall be privileged . . . to become privy to details of history and doctrine found only on the large plates of Nephi."[34]

So incomplete is the present revelation of scripture in the *Book of Mormon, Doctrine and Covenants,* and the *Pearl of Great Price* that instead of carrying these, Mormons in the millennium "may need to pull little red wagons brimful with books."[35] Not only does this view teach that there is final and authoritative truth outside of the Bible, but there is extra-Mormon scriptural truth that will only be discovered in the millennium. Secretive and magical are the best ways to describe the Mormon view of both the millennium and scripture.

What will conditions be like? Paradise will be restored. Satan will be bound, righteous government will rule, no disease will exist, and even the animal kingdom "will live together in harmony."[36]

After the end of the thousand years, Satan will be loosed for a short time. He will attempt to establish his authority. Having regathered his armies, Satan will attack the hosts of heaven under the leadership of Michael (or Adam). In this conflict, Satan will be defeated and "cast out forever."[37]

FINAL JUDGMENT AND THE END

All of the people of the earth, as is the case in the Bible, will be gathered for a final judgment. In this great assembly, "people will be assigned to the kingdoms they will have prepared for by the way they have lived." And then "the earth will be changed into a celestial kingdom."[38]

Who will judge? "The son" is the answer of Mormonism, but much more is added to the Bible than the Christian view. Jesus "in turn, will call upon others to assist in the judgment."[39] "The Twelve" apostles will help in assessing the spiritual status of the "twelve tribes of Israel." But the "Nephite twelve," who oversaw the affairs of the people of the *Book of Mormon,* "will judge the Nephite and Lamanite people" of that period. (Beyond the ranks of Mormons themselves, no scholar believes these people existed.) Finally, LDS Church literature claims that "the First Presidency and the Twelve Apostles in our own dispensation will also judge us."[40]

According to their good works, then, people will inherit different degrees of glory—celestial, terrestrial, or telestial. The chapter on salvation describes the nature of the three kingdoms of glory. Remember that it is only in the celestial kingdom that a person may advance to godhood and be in the "Heavenly Father's presence." The terrestrial kingdom is where a righteous person enjoys the company of Jesus, and the telestial kingdom provides fellowship with the Holy Ghost. "Outer darkness"—"not a degree of glory"—is reserved for those "who had testimonies of Jesus through the Holy Ghost and knew the power of the Lord but allowed Satan to overcome them." According to Mormonism, these apostates, or ex-Mormons, will not receive forgiveness. Instead, "they will live in eternal darkness, torment, and misery with Satan and his angels forever."[41]

Mormons are exhorted to prepare now for the judgment to come. They say "every day is a day of judgment. We speak, think, and act according to celestial, terrestrial, or telestial law."[42]

A unique and unbiblical concept of Mormonism, however, is that even the dead can work and prepare themselves for a better judgment for the world to come. The Bible is very explicit that after death comes judgment (Heb. 9:27). Life is our opportunity to exercise faith in Christ and, out of gratitude to him, to serve him unselfishly. For Mormonism, on the other hand, death brings one to the "postmortal spirit world" full of opportunities to better oneself prior to the final judgment.

THE SPIRIT WORLD

According to LDS teaching, the spirit world is the place of existence for the souls of the dead. It consists of two divisions or states: paradise and spirit prison. Paradise is "a state of rest," peace, or happiness for the "spirits of those who are righteous."[43] Spirits there "are occupied in doing the work of the Lord," or more accurately, the work of the LDS Church. Messengers are sent from paradise to spirit prison to "carry the light of the gospel [ordinances of the LDS Church] to them that were in darkness, to the disobedient spirits."[44]

Interestingly, the spirit world is organized along the lines of the Mormon movement: "The Church is organized in the spirit world, with each prophet standing at the head of his own generation. Priesthood holders continue their responsibilities in the spirit world. Every Apostle, every seventy, every elder, etc., who has died in the faith as soon as he passes to the other side of the veil, enters into the work of the ministry."[45]

The Mormon Church is transposed and continues its full role in the next world. Spirit prison holds "the spirits of those who have not yet received the gospel of Jesus Christ." In this postmortem existence, Mormonism teaches that these spirits must be "enticed" by both good and evil. They may accept "the gospel" (laws and ordinances of Mormonism) and "the ordinances performed for them in the temples." That is, if someone is baptized and married by proxy in a Mormon temple for them, they may accept it and thereby "prepare themselves to leave the spirit prison and dwell in paradise."[46]

Paradise is a type of probationary existence, much like the Catholic idea of purgatory. But people who "rejected the gospel . . . on earth or in the spirit prison" suffer "in a condition known as hell." Hell for the Mormon is not eternal. Unbelievers "after suffering in full for their sins . . . will be allowed to inherit the lowest degree of glory"—the telestial kingdom. "Even the spirits who have committed the greatest sins will have suffered sufficiently by the end of the Millennium."[47] Outer darkness is eternal but is reserved only for LDS apostates, the devil, and his angels.

MORMONISM AND THE END TIMES

Mormonism uses biblical terms, expressions, and concepts in its teaching on end times and the afterlife. It adds significantly to the Bible by exalting the role of the LDS Church as an exact expression of the kingdom of God. Obedience to the Church and the place of Mormon Church officials as the governors of the spiritual or post-mortal realm are all nonbiblical.

The most serious error of Mormonism, however, is its claim that in the postmortal or spirit world one may achieve salvation or a higher level of heaven. The Bible is clear that it is appointed unto humankind to die and then be judged once. Knowing Jesus Christ and experiencing the forgiveness of sin through his death on the cross is, according to Christian Scripture, the only way to salvation.

WITNESSING POINTS

- Remember that the final judgment for a Mormon is related to one's position in the LDS Church. The most dutiful Mormons are exalted to the celestial kingdom.

- The Mormon Church believes that it is the only true church and that it will reign supreme by the end of the millennium.

- Mormons think salvation will come for many non-Mormons by their suffering in spirit prison before and during the millennium. Non-Mormons will then gain the telestial kingdom.

- According to the LDS Church, many non-Mormons will gain the terrestrial kingdom due to their good deeds.

- Emphasize that the Bible endorses none of the above claims.

- Point out that Christians believe Jesus Christ is King of kings and Lord of lords and is the sole judge at the end of time.

- Show that the Bible says ultimate salvation is based on grace alone through faith, not on our good works.

MORMON ESCHATOLOGY	CHRISTIAN ESCHATOLOGY
Mormons believe that Jesus will come to Mormon leadership in his first appearance at the end of times.	The Bible teaches that Jesus will not show favoritism to any church or cult but will manifest himself as Savior to Christians when he returns.
Mormons believe that the *Book of Mormon, Doctrine and Covenants,* and *Pearl of Great Price* are the best and final sources of truth about the end times.	Christians believe that the Bible alone is the only source of truth about the end of the world and the second coming.
Mormons believe in three definite levels of glory—celestial, terrestrial, and telestial.	Christians believe that every believer will dwell in the same heaven in the presence of the Father, Son, and Holy Spirit.
Mormons teach that the establishment of the LDS Church and the production of the *Book of Mormon* are a fulfillment of the prophecy of the spread of the gospel in the end times.	The Bible teaches that the worldwide spread of the gospel in its biblical form is a sign of the end.
Mormonism equates the growth of the LDS Church with the growth of the kingdom of God.	The Bible sees the growth of the kingdom of God as the reception of Jesus Christ by people everywhere.
Mormons see themselves as literally and historically descended from Israel.	The Bible speaks of historical Israel as the Jewish people and spiritual Israel as the church.

MORMON ESCHATOLOGY	CHRISTIAN ESCHATOLOGY
Mormonism believes that the presidents and leaders of the church will help to judge people of their generation.	The Bible teaches Christ only judges on the issue of salvation. While the Scripture makes a few references to Christians judging angels, no other facts are known.
Mormonism teaches that Joseph Smith and other resurrected beings will help to rule the earth during the millennium.	The Bible teaches that Christ will reign along with his true saints regardless of their church identity.
Mormonism teaches that in the afterlife one may advance from spirit prison to paradise and in the resurrection receive a "greater glory" than what they merited from their earthly life.	Christianity teaches that earthly life is the preparation for salvation and eternal rewards.

Chapter 9
BY WHOSE AUTHORITY?

he Mormon Church teaches that when Christ set up
the true church, he ordained twelve men as apostles
and gave them the necessary priesthood authority to
act in the name of God. Mormons believe that after
the death of the apostles, some leaders began to introduce
false doctrines into the early Christian church. Because of
this apostasy, God removed the priesthood from the earth.
Without this priesthood authority, no one could rightfully
lead the church, ordain men to various offices, or baptize
new members. Thus, the true church came to an end.

This so-called total apostasy lasted until 1829 when
Joseph Smith claimed that John the Baptist appeared to

him and Oliver Cowdery and ordained them to the Aaronic Priesthood. A month later, the apostles Peter, James, and John appeared to Smith and Cowdery and ordained them to the Melchizedek Priesthood. With this authority Smith was able to restore the true Church in 1830.

LDS apostle James E. Talmage explained the Mormon position: "'Mormonism' affirms that such restoration was a necessity, inasmuch as mankind had fallen away from the Gospel of Christ during the dark ages of history, with the inevitable consequence that the *Holy Priesthood* had been taken from the earth, and *authority* to administer the essential and saving ordinances of the Gospel *had been lost*" (emphasis added).[1] The LDS Church teaches that even God operates by this eternal priesthood authority.[2]

THE MORMON PRIESTHOOD

There are two divisions in the Mormon priesthood: the Aaronic and the Melchizedek.[3] The Aaronic Priesthood operates under the authority of the Melchizedek Priesthood and has three offices: deacon, teacher, and priest.

A deacon is a Mormon boy, usually ordained at age twelve, who assists in passing the Sacrament each Sunday, helps with ushering, and does such various assignments as collecting monthly offerings for the poor. A teacher is a young man who has usually advanced to this office when he is fourteen. Two of his main duties are visiting the members and assisting in the preparation of the Sacrament. The next advancement in the priesthood is at the age of sixteen, when the young man becomes a priest. He may assist with baptisms, administer the Sacrament, and ordain other priests, teachers, and deacons.

Presiding over these offices is the bishop (leader of a local congregation). One of Joseph Smith's revelations acknowledged that only a man who is "a literal descendant of Aaron" could hold the office of bishop. But if no such descendant could be found, then the office could be filled by a high priest from the Melchizedek Priesthood,[4] which consists of several offices: elder, high priest, patriarch, seventy, and apostle.

If a young man has been faithful in the Aaronic Priesthood, he could be advanced to elder at the age of eighteen. All Melchizedek Priesthood holders are elders. They are to oversee the spiritual work of the church, including such duties as teaching, conducting church meetings, baptizing, ordaining, and anointing the sick. Most LDS men are elders.

The high priest conducts various meetings. One LDS manual states, "Stake presidents, mission presidents, high councilors, bishoprics, and other leaders of the Church are ordained high priests."[5]

One patriarch is in each stake (geographical area comprised of several congregations known as wards). His function is to give patriarchal blessings or special prayers to the members.

The Quorum of Seventy serves under the twelve apostles. A seventy is involved in missionary outreach and church growth.

At the head of the LDS Church is a First Presidency consisting of three men; each is an apostle. Besides these three, there is a quorum of twelve apostles. They are the top priesthood leaders in the church. The apostle with the most seniority is the president of the church.

The LDS Church separates itself from all other churches, claiming that its leaders have the sole right to minister by God's priesthood authority. LDS apostle Bruce R. McConkie explained the necessity of the priesthood: "If there is no *Melchizedek Priesthood* on earth, the true Church is not here and *the gospel of Christ is not available to men*. But where the Melchizedek Priesthood is, there is the kingdom, the Church, and the fulness of the gospel. . . . Perfection can be gained only in and through and because of this priesthood. . . . God on his part agrees to give such persons an inheritance of exaltation and godhood in his everlasting presence" (emphasis added).[6]

The sixth Article of Faith of the LDS Church states, "We believe in the same organization that existed in the Primitive Church, viz., apostles, prophets, pastors, teachers, evangelists, etc."[7] Since the Mormon Church makes the specific claim that their priesthood is the same as the New Testament church, we need to compare their offices with those mentioned in the Bible.

CONTRASTS WITH THE
BIBLICAL PRIESTHOOD

The Aaronic Priesthood of the Old Testament was restricted to
Aaron's descendants, who were of the tribe of Levi (Num. 3:1–10;
8:5–22; Exod. 38:21). Mormons do not claim to be descended
from Aaron. Many of them claim to be descended from the tribe of
Ephraim, but this would not make them eligible for the Aaronic
Priesthood. Even Jesus could not hold the Aaronic Priesthood
because he descended from the tribe of Judah. Hebrews 7:14
explains, "For *it is* evident that our Lord arose from Judah, of
which tribe Moses spoke nothing concerning priesthood."

The priesthood of the Old Testament was brought to an end
with the death of Christ. "Therefore, if perfection were by the Levitical priesthood (for under it the people received the law), what further need *was there* that another priest should rise according to the
order of Melchizedek, and not be called according to the order of
Aaron? For the priesthood being changed, of necessity there is also
a change of the law" (Heb. 7:11–12). Also, God set the minimum
age of the Aaronic Priesthood at twenty-five (Num. 8:23–25),
while the Mormons ordain a boy at the age of twelve.

Melchizedek is mentioned in Genesis 14:17–20 as the King of
Salem (Jerusalem) and priest of God who blessed Abraham. In
Psalm 110:4, a promise was given that his priesthood would be forever. That promise was fulfilled in Jesus Christ as indicated in
chapters 5 through 7 of Hebrews where Melchizedek is identified
as a type of Christ. Christ is the only one "after the order of
Melchizedek." He is our superior priest. "And having been perfected, He became the author of eternal salvation to all who obey
him, called by God as High Priest *'according to the order of
Melchizedek,'* . . . who has come, not according to the law of a
fleshly commandment, but according to the power of an endless
life. . . . But He, because He continues forever, has an unchangeable
priesthood" (Heb. 5:9–10; 7:16, 24).

The only Christian priesthood mentioned in the New Testament is the spiritual priesthood of every believer. Peter wrote, "you
also, as living stones, are being built up a spiritual house, a holy

priesthood, to offer up spiritual sacrifices acceptable to God through Jesus Christ. . . . But you are a chosen generation, a royal priesthood, a holy nation, His own special people" (1 Pet. 2:5, 9). Notice that males are not singled out as the only ones holding this priesthood. It is for every Christian.

High Priest

Only one Jewish high priest was appointed at a time. He was not replaced until his death. Because Christ lives forever, his priesthood can never pass to another. When Paul gave instructions to Timothy about leadership, he did not mention anything about ordaining men to either the Aaronic or Melchizedek priesthoods. Instead, the emphasis was on choosing mature Christians: "And the things that you have heard from me among many witnesses, commit these to faithful men who will be able to teach others also" (2 Tim. 2:2).

Hebrews 5:1 explains that the duties of the Jewish high priest were to "offer both gifts and sacrifices for sins." Mormon high priests do not offer any sacrifices, so they are not following the Old Testament pattern.

The Jewish high priest served as a "copy and shadow of heavenly things" (Heb. 8:5). Christ fulfilled the priestly duties "once for all when He offered up Himself" (Heb. 7:22–27). He is the only high priest in the Christian church. No verses in the New Testament refer to any Christian holding the office of high priest.

Priests

In the LDS Church a young man is ordained a priest in the Aaronic Priesthood at the age of sixteen and does not need to be a descendant of Aaron. Such a thing was never done in the Old Testament. The New Testament mentions Jewish priests, but an office of priest is never mentioned in the Christian church.

Apostles and Prophets

In Mormonism the president of the church is considered a prophet and apostle. LDS apostle Bruce R. McConkie stated, "Apostles and prophets are the foundation upon which the organization of the true Church rests."

In trying to establish the need for apostles and prophets in the church, Mormons appeal to 1 Corinthians 12:28: "And God has appointed these in the church: first apostles, second prophets, third teachers, after that miracles, then gifts of healings, helps, administrations, varieties of tongues." However, if one reads the entire section from verse 27 to verse 31, it is obvious that Paul is discussing various ministries or gifts in the early church, not listing specific offices of the priesthood.

Notice also that Paul lists apostles first and prophets second, indicating their order of importance. In Mormonism the highest calling is the prophet of the church; apostles serve under him. This is a reversal of the biblical order. Also, in Mormonism, teachers are fourteen-year-old boys, not men third in rank to the prophet and apostles.

After Judas betrayed Christ, there was one man chosen to replace him in the twelve apostles (Acts 1:21-23). To qualify for this position, the person had to be an eyewitness to the full ministry of Jesus, including his resurrection. The New Testament offers no evidence that others were later chosen to take the place of anyone else in the twelve. Due to the requirements given in Acts, this process could not continue past the first generation of Christians.

Another problem for the LDS position is the concept of having three apostles in its First Presidency to oversee the twelve apostles. This would add up to fifteen apostles and would not be the same as Jesus' twelve apostles. If Mormonism is going to insist that the church today must be set up exactly like it was under Christ, then they have too many apostles. The Mormons cannot have it both ways. Either they are a "restoration" that is exactly like the New Testament church, or they are setting up something different from the early Christian church.

Bishops and Elders

In 1 Timothy 3:1 and Titus 1:7, the word *bishop* appears in the King James Version of the Bible. But in the New International Version, it is translated *overseer*. Many Bible scholars have concluded from these passages that, in the New Testament at least, bishop is not a separate office in the church but one of the elders.

Deacons

The LDS Church ordains twelve-year-old boys to the office of deacon. The Bible, however, states they are to be mature men and "the husbands of one wife" (1 Tim. 3:8–12), qualifications twelve-year-olds could not meet.

Teachers

In the LDS Church a boy is made a teacher at the age of fourteen. This is supposed to be a part of the Aaronic Priesthood. However, the New Testament passages about teachers do not make them part of a special priesthood. Also, teachers were to be mature Christians "able to teach others," not teenagers (2 Tim. 2:2).

Pastors

Mormons will often use Ephesians 4:11 when trying to prove their system of priesthood. This verse reads, "And He Himself gave some to be apostles, and some prophets, some evangelists, and some pastors and teachers." The LDS Church, however, does not have any pastors. One of their apostles explained their position: "The term pastor does not refer to an order in the priesthood, like deacon, priest, elder . . . a bishop is a pastor; so is an elder who has charge of a branch."[8] It is inconsistent for Mormons to insist the words *apostles* and *teachers* are specific offices of the priesthood, while denying that *pastor* or *evangelist* are priesthood offices.

Evangelist or Patriarch

Another problem with the LDS use of Ephesians 4:11 is the mention of evangelists. No such office is in the Mormon Church. Instead, they claim that the original meaning has been lost and that an evangelist is supposed to be a patriarch. One of their apostles explained: "An evangelist is a patriarch. . . . The Patriarch to the Church holds the keys of blessing for the members of the Church."[9] LDS apostle Bruce R. McConkie claimed, "Having lost the true knowledge of the priesthood and its offices, . . . the false traditions of the sectarian world have applied the designation evangelist to traveling preachers, missionaries, and revivalists."[10]

Despite the LDS claim, there is no evidence that the Greek word *evangelist* ever carried the meaning of patriarch. The Greek word translated *evangelist* carries the meaning of someone who proclaims the good news, not one who gives prayer blessings to church members. In the LDS Church a patriarchal blessing is given to the members as a sort of spiritual blueprint for their lives.[11]

Seventy

In the Mormon Church, a seventy is a special type of missionary and overseer of a specific area of the church.[12] Joseph Smith evidently read about Christ sending out seventy men in Luke 10:1 and turned this event into an ordination of men into a specific office of the priesthood. However, the New Testament does not mention anyone ever being appointed to be a replacement for any of these men. Surely if such an office was to be part of the church, it would have been mentioned somewhere in the New Testament, particularly in Acts or the pastoral epistles.

Paid Ministry

In both the Old and New Testaments those who served the Lord full-time were compensated from the tithes and offerings of the people. When the Levitical priesthood was originally established, God made provision for the support of the priests. "Levites, one tribe out of the Twelve, were set apart for the work of God. God took them, in lieu of First-Born sons. . . . *They were supported by Tithes;* and had 48 cities (Num. 35:7; Josh. 21:19). One Family of Levites, Aaron and Sons, were set apart to be Priests. The Rest of the Levites were to be Assistants to the Priests" (emphasis added).[13]

The practice of a paid ministry was continued in the New Testament church. Paul instructed Timothy: "Let the elders who rule well be counted worthy of double honor, especially those who labor in the word and doctrine. For the Scripture says, *'You shall not muzzle an ox while it treads out the grain,'* and, 'The laborer is worthy of his wages'" (1 Tim. 5:17–18). While Paul sometimes labored with his own hands, he stated that he had the right to ask for support from fellow Christians. Paul wrote to the church at Corinth: "Do we have no right to take along a believing wife, as do also the other apostles, the brothers of the Lord, and Cephas? Or is it only Barnabas and I who have no right to refrain from working?" (1 Cor. 9:5–6). Further on in the same letter, Paul wrote: "If we have sown spiritual things for you, is it a great thing if we reap your material things? . . . Even so the Lord has commanded that those who preach the gospel should live from the gospel" (1 Cor. 9:11, 14).

In Paul's second letter to the church at Corinth, he again raises the issue of his support. He states that when he was among them they did not give him financial support, but he received it from other churches: "I robbed other churches, taking wages from them to minister to you" (2 Cor. 11:8). When Paul wrote to the church at Philippi, he acknowledged their financial support: "For even in Thessalonica you sent *aid* once and again for my necessities. . . . I am full, having received from Epaphroditus the things *sent* from you, a sweet-smelling aroma, an acceptable sacrifice, well pleasing to God" (Phil. 4:16, 18).

The LDS Church boasts of not having a paid clergy. Many of them believe that when a man receives a salary from a particular group, it compromises his integrity. One convert to Mormonism stated his belief this way: "The meetings are not dominated by one individual, such as a priest, rabbi or minister. Everyone participates. The Mormon Church has no paid clergy. This permits free expression and the fear of losing one's job is not present. How important this is can be judged by one who has seen the clergy of other faiths *prostitute themselves* for the jobs they hold" (emphasis added).[14] LDS apostle Boyd K. Packer explained, "In the Church of Jesus Christ of Latter-day Saints there is no paid ministry, no professional clergy, as is common in other churches."[15]

Even though leaders on the local level receive no pay for their services, this is not true of the top leadership. Many of the Mormons are not aware that their apostles receive a salary. The *Encyclopedia of Mormonism* states this practice: "Because the Church has no professional clergy, it is administered at every level through LAY

PARTICIPATION AND LEADERSHIP, and officials other than the General Authorities contribute their time and talents without remuneration. . . . Because the General Authorities are obliged to leave their regular employment for full-time Church service, they receive a modest living allowance provided from income on Church investments."[16] Since the Mormon Church concedes the right to pay those who serve in a full-time capacity, we are left to wonder why they have such strong objections to ministers receiving a "modest living allowance."

Another puzzling aspect of Mormonism is that there is no accounting to the membership of church funds. They are never informed as to the amount of the "modest living allowance" given to their top leaders. In Christian churches the financial statement is a matter of public record. There is no guesswork as to the amount a local congregation pays its minister.

Baptism

The LDS Church believes that baptism by the proper priesthood authority is necessary for it to be valid and to admit one to the true church and the highest level of heaven. As LDS apostle Bruce R. McConkie said:

> Baptism by immersion under the hands of a legal administrator, one empowered to bind on earth and seal in heaven, is the initiatory ordinance into the Church on earth and the celestial kingdom in the world to come. . . . Baptism serves four purposes: 1. It is for the remission of sins. . . . 2. It admits the repentant person to membership in the Church and kingdom of God on earth. . . . 3. It is the gate to the celestial kingdom of heaven, that is, it starts a person out on the straight and narrow path which leads to eternal life. . . . 4. It is the means whereby the door to personal sanctification is opened. . . . He [Christ] had to be baptized to gain admission to the celestial kingdom.[17]

The LDS Church does not recognize any baptisms other than those performed by its priesthood. Mormonism has redefined the words *saved, baptism, heaven, eternal life,* and *presence of God.* They believe one can be saved (go to one of the lower levels of heaven) but not have eternal life (exaltation, godhood, and life in the presence of God). For a person to gain admittance to the celestial (top) kingdom of heaven, he or she must be baptized by one holding the LDS priesthood.

While the Bible speaks of believers being baptized, it never states it has to be done by someone holding a special priesthood. The emphasis is on believing, not priesthood authority. The Philippian jailer asked Paul and Silas, "Sirs, what must I do to be saved?" They responded, "Believe on the Lord Jesus Christ, and you will be saved, you and your household." Then "he and all his family were baptized." He then "rejoiced, having believed in God" (Acts 16:30–34). Baptism, while an act of obedience, is but a symbol of one's identification with Christ and is not a necessary requirement for salvation.

LDS TEMPLE CEREMONIES

One of the most important tenants of the LDS Church is the necessity of temple ordinances. The LDS Church teaches that those with proper priesthood authority only can administer these essential rites. Joseph Smith supposedly restored the original temple ceremony of the Old Testament.

More than fifty LDS temples are in operation today, with a number in the planning stage. LDS apostle Bruce R. McConkie explained the importance of temples: "From the days of Adam to the present, whenever the Lord has had a people on earth, temples and temple ordinances have been a crowning feature of their worship. . . . The inspired erection and proper use of temples is one of the great evidences of the divinity of the Lord's work. . . . Where these are not, the Church and kingdom and the truth of heaven are not."[18]

The LDS temples are used for eternal marriages for both the living and the dead, as well as baptisms for the dead. Young people usually perform proxy baptisms. When adult Mormons attend the temple, they go through the ceremony only once themselves. After that, they will attend the temple on behalf of a dead person of the same sex. The live Mormon stands in the place of a particular dead person and goes through the entire endowment ceremony in that person's name.

A person must have a temple marriage to progress to godhood. These ordinances are kept secret and are never to be discussed outside of the temple.

When Mormons reach adulthood, they are encouraged to go to the temple to "take out their endowments." LDS president Brigham Young taught that this meant receiving key words and signs: "Your endowment is, to receive all those ordinances in the House of the Lord, which are necessary for you, after you have departed this life, to enable you to walk back to the presence of the Father, passing the angels who stand as sentinels, being enabled to give them the key words, the signs and tokens, pertaining to the Holy Priesthood, and gain your eternal exaltation in spite of earth and hell."[19]

This temple ceremony is necessary before a person serves a full-time mission. A person must go to his or her bishop and receive a "recommend," a special certificate that shows the person is in good standing in the LDS Church. The person then attends a special ceremony at the temple.

Upon arrival, the men and women go to separate locker rooms. There they change out of their street clothes and put on a white covering, something like a poncho. Each person then goes to a special booth where attendants of the same sex anoint the person's body with oil and water, repeating various prayers, and then assist the person with putting on the new temple underwear.

This garment, produced by the LDS Church, is available in both one- and two-piece styles. The man's is usually of cotton and the woman's of nylon material. On the breast of all styles are small embroidery stitches that form the pattern of a compass and square and look like a small letter *L* and *V*. These symbols were taken from Freemasonry. The garment is to be worn day and night, except for bathing and athletics. After the person dresses in this garment, he or she puts on a white outfit, hat or veil, and slippers. The person carries a small bundle containing a green apron and white robe to be worn later in the ceremony.

Everyone then goes to the main temple auditorium room where a film dramatizing the creation is shown. This film depicts Elohim (God the Father), Jehovah (Jesus), and Michael (Adam) as they jointly go through the six days of creation. Then Michael becomes Adam. After showing the creation of Eve, the film demonstrates Adam and Eve's fall.

After the film each person is instructed in special handshakes and passwords that are necessary to gain admittance into the celestial kingdom. Smith borrowed these handshakes and passwords from Freemasonry when he invented his ceremony. The person also swears to always support the church in everything.

After this part of the rite, those who are getting married for eternity, or performing a proxy marriage for eternity, go into different smaller rooms for the actual marriage ceremony. Everyone then returns to the locker rooms to dress in their street clothes, with their temple garments on underneath.[20]

The LDS Church teaches that since these ceremonies are necessary to gain admittance to the presence of God, they should also be performed for those who died without a chance to join Mormonism. This is why the Mormons have such extensive genealogical libraries. They believe they must trace everyone's lineage back as far as possible and be baptized and married by proxy for all those who did not have a chance to hear their gospel. The Bible has no such teaching.

If Paul understood the need for temple marriages for the dead, it is strange he would write the following instructions to his fellow workers Timothy and Titus: "Nor give heed to fables and endless genealogies, which cause disputes rather than godly edification" (1 Tim. 1:4). "But avoid foolish disputes, and genealogies, contentions, and strivings about the law; for they are unprofitable and useless" (Titus 3:9).

When trying to establish the need for baptizing the dead, Mormons use 1 Corinthians 15:29: "Otherwise what will they do who are baptized for the dead, if the dead rise not at all? Why then are they baptized for the dead?" This is the only verse in the Bible that mentions baptism for the dead. Notice that Paul is not advocating this practice. He merely makes a passing reference to some group that had such a practice. His emphasis throughout that chapter is on the resurrection. Had baptism for the dead been a primary function of the early church, surely there would be more teaching on it than this casual reference. Contrast this to Joseph Smith's emphasis: "The greatest responsibility in this world that God has laid upon us, is to seek after our dead."[21] If such is the case, it is certainly strange that the Bible has only one obscure verse that mentions baptism for the dead and two verses that condemn genealogies.

The LDS temple endowments and other rites are not based on biblical teaching. The temple in the Old Testament, with its high priest and animal sacrifices, was a foreshadowing of Christ's role as both our final High Priest and last blood offering for sin (Heb. chaps. 5–9). When Christ died on the cross, the veil of the temple was torn apart (Luke 23:45), thus signifying that the Old Testament temple ritual had been replaced by the atonement of Christ.

Eternal Marriage

There is nothing in the New Testament about "eternal marriages" and secret rituals in a Christian temple. The Jewish temple ceremonies are clearly explained in the Old Testament (Exod. chaps. 26–30) and have no relationship to the LDS temple ceremony.

The only eternal marriage in the Bible is the spiritual marriage of the believer to Christ. Paul wrote to the Christians at Corinth, "I have betrothed you to one husband [Christ], that I may present you [the Christians] as a chaste virgin to Christ" (2 Cor. 11:2). Paul also wrote in Romans 7:4 that Christians are to be "married to another—to Him [Christ] who is raised from the dead, that we should bear fruit to God." This is a spiritual union, not an actual marriage.

Christ never mentions the need for an eternal marriage. In fact, he taught just the opposite: "The children of this world marry, and are given in marriage: But they which shall be accounted worthy to obtain that world, and the resurrection from the dead, neither marry, nor are given in marriage: Neither can they die any more: for they are equal unto the angels; and are the children of God" (Luke 20:34–36 KJV). Notice that Christ equated those who are not married in heaven with "the children of God." Christians look forward to being with their loved ones in heaven. As brothers and sisters in Christ, we will be together as one large family, the family of God. However, there is nothing in the Bible to show that this would include marriage relationships.

Special Temples

There is nothing in the Bible to indicate that Christians were to build temples. Some of the early Jewish Christians met in the courtyard of the temple in Jerusalem for prayer, but they certainly were not performing any rites like the Mormon ceremony. The New Testament teaches that God's temple is a spiritual building made up of all Christians, with Christ as the foundation (1 Cor. 3:16). This is emphasized in Ephesians 2:19–22: "Now, therefore, you are no longer strangers . . . but fellow citizens with the saints and members of the household of God, having been built on the foundation of the apostles and prophets, Jesus Christ Himself being the chief cornerstone, in whom all the whole building, being fitted together, grows into a holy temple in the Lord, in whom you also are being built together for a dwelling place of God in the Spirit."

False Prophets

Mormons will usually say they know Joseph Smith is a prophet of God because they prayed about it and received a spiritual confirmation of his teachings. But is this the proper way to determine if his message is truly from God? The Bible never says to test a prophet by prayer, but by his message. Deuteronomy 13 warns that a prophet must teach correctly about God. Chapter 18 tells us the prophet's prophecies must come to pass. Paul gave a severe warning against false teachings in Galatians 1:8: "But even if we, or an angel from heaven, preach any other gospel to you than what we have preached to you, let him be accursed."

We are to compare a person's message with the teachings of the apostles. When Paul went to Berea to proclaim Jesus as the Messiah to the Jews, the people there demonstrated the correct procedure: "These were more fair-minded than those in Thessalonica, in that

BY WHOSE AUTHORITY?

149

they received the word with all readiness, and searched the Scriptures daily to find out whether these things were so. Therefore many of them believed" (Acts 17:11–12). Paul did not tell them to go home and pray about it. They were praised for searching the Scriptures, in other words, testing the message to see if it agreed with the prophecies of the Messiah.

Note that John made an appeal to fact, not feeling, when he declared, "That which was from the beginning, which we have heard, which we have seen with our eyes, which we have looked upon, and our hands have handled, concerning the Word of life . . . that which we have seen and heard we declare to you, that you also may have fellowship with us" (1 John 1:1, 3).

Peter also reminded the recipients of his second letter about the basis for Christian beliefs: "For we did not follow cunningly devised fables . . . but were eyewitnesses of His majesty. For He received from God the Father honor and glory when such a voice came to Him from the Excellent Glory: 'This is My beloved Son . . .' And we heard this voice which came from heaven when we were with Him on the holy mountain. And so we have the prophetic word confirmed" (2 Pet. 16–19).

John urged his readers not to be gullible: "Beloved, do not believe every spirit, but test the spirits, whether they are of God; because many false prophets have gone out into the world" (1 John 4:1).

And Peter wrote specifically to warn about false teachers: "But there were false prophets also among the people, even as there shall be false teachers among you, who privily shall bring in damnable heresies, . . . And many shall follow their pernicious ways" (2 Pet. 2:1–2 KJV). He wanted Christians to remember what they had learned after he was gone: "I now write to you this second epistle (in *both* of which I stir up your pure minds by way of reminder), that you may be mindful of the words which were spoken before by the holy prophets, and of the commandment of us, the apostles of the Lord and Savior, knowing this first: that scoffers will come in the last days" (2 Pet. 3:1–3). Notice Peter referred them to past teachings and facts, not to feelings or prayer.

In contrast, the Mormons cite James 1:5: "If any of you lacks wisdom, let him ask of God," when encouraging people to pray for a testimony. But that verse actually refers to asking for wisdom during times of temptation and persecution, not for knowledge or testing of a prophet. James goes on to warn those who pray for the wrong things: "You ask and do not receive, because you ask amiss" (James 4:3). This verse shows that we can pray about and ask for wrong things. If someone claimed God said we should rob a bank and give the money to the poor, would we need to pray about it? No! God has already spoken on the issue in the Ten Commandments.

Why should we pray to know if Joseph Smith is a prophet or if his teachings are from God? The Bible says to test the prophet's message by what God has already spoken. When this test is applied to Joseph Smith, he stands condemned as a false prophet. Certainly a decision regarding our eternal life is the most important one we will ever make and deserves a careful biblical examination.

WITNESSING POINTS

- Remember that the LDS Church claims to have the one true Church and that only through participation in it can people experience the "fullness of salvation."
- Baptism in the Church of Jesus Christ of Latter-day Saints is considered the only true baptism. In their opinion it must be administered by LDS priesthood holders.
- The two priesthoods, Aaronic and Melchizedek, are not New Testament offices apart from the work of Christ.
- The LDS Church does not exercise the biblical office of pastor and mistakenly reinterprets the biblical roles of patriarch, evangelist, and apostle.
- Point your LDS friend to Christ and away from trust in any church for salvation.

Chapter 10

MEETING THE MORMON CHALLENGE

H oney . . . would you get the door?" called Sue Murray from the kitchen one Saturday morning.

Joe ambled from the family room and opened the front door.

"Good day, sir! My name is John Harris and this is Ron Harper. I'm pastor of Riverside Church on Main Street. We're in the neighborhood this morning inviting people to attend a revival at our church next week. Do you have a church you attend?"

"Uh . . . yes," Joe said. "We recently joined the Church of Jesus Christ of Latter-day Saints."

"That's interesting," Pastor John said. "How did you come to join that church?"

"Well, my wife wanted to go to church, and I saw that they were giving away free Bibles. So we called and ordered one. Two LDS missionaries came to our house to deliver it."

By this time Sue, holding their new baby boy, had joined them at the door. "That's right," she said. "We were really impressed by their testimony, so we began to study with them. We learned a lot we had never known before about God and Jesus. We visited the local ward and liked it. So a couple of months ago we decided to be baptized and join."

"So you weren't raised Mormons?" Pastor John said. "Were you Christians before?"

"Sort of," Joe said. "We both went to church when we were kids."

"I went regularly when I was a teenager," Sue explained. "But I had gotten away from God until I met the Mormons. And we wanted a good start for our family." She jogged the tiny bundle in her arms and pulled back the corner of the blanket so the men could see the baby's face.

"How precious!" Pastor John smiled, stroking the baby's fingers. Then he looked at Sue. "I'm curious. Did the Mormons ask you about your personal relationship with Christ?"

"What do you mean?" Sue asked.

"Did they ask you if you knew him as your personal Savior and Lord?"

"Well, I suppose so. They told us about how he's our spiritual brother and the literal Son of the heavenly Father. They said he suffered and died to restore immortality to God's children. They said we come to him by joining his restored church."

"Did it seem to you that what they said was unusual, at least compared to what you had learned in church as a child?" Pastor John asked.

"No, not really," Sue said. "I think they helped us understand more clearly about God's plan and what Jesus has done for us."

"Would it surprise you," Pastor John paused and smiled, "if I were to tell you that what the LDS teaches and believes is very different from what other Christian churches believe?"

"Oh, we know there are some differences," Joe said. "But basically we believe the same things, don't we?"

"I've studied the teachings of the LDS Church for many years," Pastor John said. "In my opinion, the differences far outweigh the similarities."

"In what ways?" Sue asked.

Pastor John carefully explained how the LDS doctrines of the nature of God, the person and work of Jesus Christ, the way of salvation, and the place of the Bible strongly differ from orthodox Christian views.

Sue and Joe looked at each other. Joe shrugged and took a step back from the open door.

"We didn't realize there were such differences between the LDS and other Christian beliefs," Sue said. "We wanted to join a good church, and they seem like such nice people with good families. They didn't go into all the things you mentioned. Are you sure it's like that?"

"Absolutely!" Pastor John said. "If I gave you some material that tells more about it, would you look at it?"

"I don't know . . ." Joe said, shaking his head. "The missionaries warned us about reading apostate literature from disgruntled ex-members."

"We're not ex-members. These pamphlets are published by our denomination. They evaluate Mormonism from a Christian perspective. Will you at least read them?"

"Well . . ." Joe scratched his head above his right ear. "All right."

Later that afternoon Pastor John stopped by the Murray's house and dropped off several pamphlets and a video tape entitled *The Mormon Puzzle: Understanding and Witnessing to Latter-day Saints.* The Murrays agreed to read the material and watch the tape.

Three days later Pastor John called and spoke to Joe. "What did you think?" he asked.

"We were shocked!" Joe said. "Sue and I really hadn't understood all that the LDS church teaches. It was eye-opening. We don't think we want to stay in that church."

Pastor John asked Joe if he could visit them again. They agreed, so the next evening he came by. They discussed the information he had given them. In the course of their conversation, he presented the simple biblical plan of salvation by grace through faith in Jesus Christ alone. The Murrays both prayed to receive Jesus as their personal Lord and Savior. Over the course of the next few weeks they asked that their names be removed from the membership roll of the LDS Church and began to attend Pastor John's church. They also began to attend a Bible study the church sponsored that helped them grow in Christ.

How do we go about the job of winning to Jesus Christ—the true Jesus of the Bible—the Sues and Joes of this world? This most important of questions requires some knowledge and planning. This chapter will focus on some general principles about evangelizing Mormons.

GENERAL PRINCIPLES

As we have seen, Mormonism is a fabricated and artificial form of Christianity. It is a new religion produced by the false prophet Joseph Smith. It teaches an unbiblical approach to salvation and insists on baptism and membership in the LDS Church to experience the fullness of heaven in the celestial kingdom. The God of Mormonism and the Jesus presented in that system are not the God and Jesus of the Bible. Therefore Paul's warning against people who preach another Jesus or teach another gospel (2 Cor. 11:4; Gal. 1:6–8) applies to the doctrinal teachings of the LDS gospel.

But genuine Bible-based Christians must do more than critique Mormonism; they must effectively witness to Mormons regarding the true gospel and urge them to believe in Jesus Christ alone for their salvation.

First of all, let's think about what evangelism is. To evangelize means merely to share the good news that Jesus Christ died for the sins of the world and that people who believe in him will be saved from all the guilt and judgment that their sins have brought them.

Salvation does not mean that a Mormon must join a particular church. Salvation is a gift. While biblical discipleship eventually involves a believer's baptism and membership in a New Testament church, the Bible teaches that faith alone in Christ saves. It saves completely and totally. God's grace makes salvation a gift to be received, not a paycheck to be earned. Mormons must understand that what we do when we share the gospel is radically different from their missionary efforts. By focusing on the following six principles, we can become effective witnesses.

Principle 1: Know the Faith

The late Walter Martin, dean and encourager of many contemporary cult-watch groups, often used an illustration regarding Secret Service agents. Agents are trained to protect key government officials and VIPs, as well as to spot counterfeiting operations. When agents are trained in spotting counterfeit bills, they are sent to the Bureau of Printing and Engraving. There, for some weeks, they learn to identify real U.S. currency. They smell it, feel it, and examine its unique visible characteristics. After several weeks of this discipline, spotting a counterfeit twenty, fifty, or hundred dollar bill is usually no problem. For a trained agent, "a counterfeit stands out like a mouse at a cat convention."

Christians, likewise, need to know the real thing—namely, the essentials of the orthodox Christian faith. The doctrines and truths about God, Jesus, the Holy Spirit, and their three-in-oneness are beautiful and real. The message of God's grace in the Bible's plan of salvation is a pearl of great and eternal value. The Bible itself has a richness of insight into God's love for us that the study efforts of a thousand lifetimes could not exhaust. Once you begin to read the Bible through, taking notes on passages that particularly speak to you, you'll be amazed that any person would need another testament of God, Jesus, or the gospel to satisfy their spiritual desires.

Here are some practical suggestions to help you begin to mine the riches of Scripture. Get a version of the Bible that you are comfortable with. Read it daily. Take notes as you read and/or underline key texts of particular meaning. Also read a good, basic book on key Bible doctrines. Look up the Bible passages when the book references them.

Write down some thoughts that will help you understand and express the Christian gospel effectively. Remember, you cannot give away what you do not possess or own for yourself. God has no grandchildren. It is only those people who know him, through faith in Jesus, and who understand his biblical plan of salvation who can genuinely call him Father.

Mormons need to encounter growing, vibrant Christians who have a grip on the key truths of the gospel. Just like a Secret Service agent, it will then become much easier to spot the counterfeit elements in Mormon claims about the LDS gospel. And this will give Mormons more opportunities to hear the truth from informed Christians.

Principle 2: Remember Mormon Doctrinal Deviance

Along with learning truth, spend some time studying the counterfeit. This book has been principally devoted to helping any person get acquainted with Mormonism's non-Christian teachings. While the LDS Church claims that it is Christian, a deeper analysis shows that it is not. Mormonism does have a Christian veneer—after all, they baptize by immersion, talk about the "gospel," and do "missionary" work—but the substance of Mormonism is not Christian. Here are five essentials to remember:

1. Mormonism claims to be the one true Church and denies that evangelical and Bible-based churches possess the "fulness of the gospel."

2. Mormonism adds to the Bible the *Book of Mormon*, the *Doctrine and Covenants*, and the *Pearl of Great Price*. LDS claim that parts of the Bible were removed and its transmission flawed. Finally, the prophet and president of the church is a living oracle of God. Whatever he teaches is to be received as the living word of God.

3. Mormonism believes in a different God than the one revealed in the Bible. The God of Mormonism was once a mortal man. He was exalted to godhood by obedience to a system similar to Mormonism. He is married to a goddess or at least a godlike wife, and he is restricted to a "body of flesh and bones."

4. Mormonism believes in a different Jesus than the one revealed through the Bible. The Jesus of LDS doctrine was born as the first of God's billions of spirit children. He is Lucifer's elder brother. At some point in the "premortal life," he became a "personage" of the godhead. He was conceived of Mary by the direct physical action of the "Heavenly Father."

5. Mormonism teaches a different gospel and plan of salvation. LDS doctrine advocates a gospel that says all people are given immortality by the death and resurrection of the Mormon Christ. Evil people must suffer for their sins in spirit prison throughout the millennium before going to the level of glory known as the telestial kingdom. "Good and righteous" persons enter the terrestrial kingdom, where they enjoy the presence of Jesus but not the heavenly Father. Those persons who would enter the celestial realm must be baptized by a priesthood holder in the LDS Church. They must also receive the Holy Ghost with the laying on of hands by the proper LDS authority. Other requirements make the celestial level of reward possible.

Is this salvation by grace? Absolutely not! Faith, trust, and belief in God's plan of salvation offered through the person and work of Christ are biblical requirements for eternal life with God, not works.

Principle 3: Clearly Define Specific Biblical Words

Mormonism uses Christian or Bible-based words, such as *gospel, atonement, salvation, eternal life, Savior, Jesus, Scriptures,* and *God.* But

Mormonism has a completely different dictionary than that of
Christians.

The glossary at the end of this book provides definitions of key
Mormon words and contrasts them with Christian meanings.
When you share the gospel with a Mormon, describe exactly what
you mean by the terms you use. For example, you might say this:
"When I talk about God, I mean the uncreated and uncaused sovereign of all the universe and of all worlds." Or, "Jesus is eternal
God; he always existed. When I call him the *Son of God,* I mean that
symbolically, not in a literal sense. Like God the Father, he is uncreated or uncaused. To know him is to know God. He came to earth
as God in the flesh." These helpful, biblical definitions will demonstrate to the Mormon the differences between their beliefs and
those of biblically centered Christians.

Be prepared for Mormons to say to you: "We believe the same
gospel as you do." Or, "We love and follow Christ just like you do.
We believe and preach the gospel as all Christians do." At a point
like that you must gently, but firmly and with clear definitions,
explain the different meanings between their use of words and
yours.

Different definitions are not unusual and need not make you
uncomfortable. When an Englishman says he wants something to
wash down his *biscuit* (a cookie) while drinking his afternoon tea,
he does not mean he wants gravy on it. When an Englishman says
his car has a big *boot* (a trunk), he does not mean that his vehicle
wears shoes. Terms and their meanings are important. When witnessing to a Mormon, it is essential to define your words.

Principle 4: Present a Clear
Testimony of Your Faith

Mormons like to give their testimonies. But they are testimonies of their belief in Joseph Smith as the prophet of God, of
Gordon B. Hinckley as the current church president, of the
truthfulness of the *Book of Mormon,* and even sometimes of the
validity of the Church of Jesus Christ of Latter-day Saints. The
Mormon testimony often is comprised of all three elements and
may sound like this: "I bear you my testimony that the *Book of*

Mormon is true and that Joseph Smith is a prophet and that the Church of Jesus Christ of Latter-day Saints is true. This is my testimony in the name of Jesus Christ. Amen."[1] Mormons may even refer to their faith, in a vague sense, in Jesus Christ.

Nonetheless, a biblically based testimony of salvation in Christ is different. A Christian focuses only on the person and work of Jesus and speaks of the certainty of his death on the cross as the atoning sacrifice for the sins of the world (John 1:29; 1 John 2:1–2). Then Christians will speak of how they were saved and came to place faith in Jesus alone—not in a church or a process of salvation by works. A changed life produced by the indwelling power of the Holy Spirit is their song. This pattern follows the biblical example of the apostle Paul's experience of saving grace (Acts 22).

Finally, the newborn believer in Christ can speak eloquently of the assurance of salvation—yes, even the fullness of God's blessings in salvation. The Bible does not speak about a first-class heaven (celestial), a coach-class heaven (the terrestrial realm), and an economy-class heaven (telestial—"a pretty nice place," as one Mormon spokesman classified it). Rather, there is one heaven where all the saints enjoy the presence of God—Father, Son, and Holy Spirit. The assurance of people saved by grace is that they will go to heaven based on their trust in Christ and his work alone. That is biblical assurance, and it is not an assurance shared by Mormons.

Think about it. If Christ did the full work of salvation, then there is no other basis for a person to believe that he or she will gain heaven except by trusting in Christ. But since the Mormon testimony is based on one's faith in Joseph Smith, the LDS Church, or the *Book of Mormon*, LDS cannot attest to, nor were they meant to be able to gain, assurance for salvation.

Remember the following three important points about the Mormons and their testimonies and sharing yours with them:

1. Assume a Mormon's testimony is sincere, although the church also knows it is used to bolster his or her confidence in such beliefs.

2. Remember a Mormon's testimony is a type of affirmation, but not a testimony of a Christ-changed life.

3. Emphasize the centrality of Jesus alone in providing the power to change one's life.

Principle 5: Warn the Mormon about Trusting in Feelings

Trusting in feelings or emotion as a means to validate the truth builds a shaky foundation. The *Book of Mormon* says, "When ye shall receive these things, I would exhort you that ye would ask God . . . in the name of Christ, if these things are not true; and if ye shall ask with a sincere heart, with real intent, having faith in Christ, he will manifest the truth of it unto you" (Moroni 10:4). *Doctrine and Covenants* 9:8 exhorts, "Study it [Mormonism] out in your mind; then you must ask me if it be right, and if it is right I will cause that your bosom shall burn within you; therefore you shall feel that it is right." This approach to validating religious truth by emotional experience is subjectivism. The problem with it is that every religion in the world has manifestations of emotion. Each one could produce witnesses who verify the truthfulness of their religion by an emotional response.

But Christianity is built upon acts of God in history that are verifiable:

- The Hebrew culture existed.
- Archaeology affirms the outline of Bible history.
- The resurrection of Jesus is verifiable.
- The spread of the early church, against insurmountable odds, was the work of the Spirit.
- The character of Christ is, according to primary documents and witnesses, spotless.
- Biblical prophecies were fulfilled and are being fulfilled.
- We have overwhelming historical and manuscript evidence of the truth of the Bible.

In fact, the closer we examine the claims of Christ, the greater our assurance grows that Jesus is who he says he is and that the Holy Bible is true.

The Mormon must tend toward having a blind faith. A close and objective view of Mormon faith, the reliability of the *Book of Mormon*, Joseph Smith's notes on the Bible, the *Doctrine and Covenants*, and the *Pearl of Great Price* generate more doubts than faith. So Mormonism relies strongly on an undefined feeling—a "burning in the bosom"—to supplant all doubt and verify all truth. In fact, Mormon leaders teach, "A testimony is to be found in the bearing of it."[2] In other words, autosuggestion or self-hypnosis through lack of conscious thought is sufficient to overcome all doubt and to contradict the evidence.

The Bible warns that we must test the spirits. It is only when "spiritual influences" confirm the Bible alone as true and Jesus as the sole sacrifice for sin and way to salvation that we know any "spirit" or its influence to be true (1 John 4:1–11; John 14:1–21). It is in living the commands of the Bible, believing the Jesus of the Bible, and doing his will that the truth is embodied in a Christian's life (John 7:16–24; 8:31–32). After all, even Satan can transform himself into an angel of light to give momentary spiritual exhilaration (2 Cor. 11:14).

Remember, a friend may claim that he is a millionaire. But if he owns no property, has no bank account, valuables, or stocks, and no cash on hand, simply feeling or hoping that he is rich is no basis for his belief that he is a millionaire.

Principle 6: Build Lasting Relationships

Mormons have been taught to expect the worst from non-Mormons. And the history of relationships between Mormon and non-Mormon, until recent decades, has bred an aura of suspicion. There have been gun battles between the two groups. Joseph Smith was killed by a lynch mob while shooting three men himself—two of whom died from their wounds. The Mountain Meadows Massacre of 1857 marks the low point between Mormons and non-Mormons. Brigham Young ordered the extermination of the male members of a "gentile" or non-

Mormon wagon train crossing Utah. Since the origin of their church, Mormon missionaries have been trained to expect the worst.

The Bible demands that Christians be different. We are not only to talk about the love of Christ, but we are also to embody it as well. The first step in doing this is to seek to understand Mormons. Just as Jesus was able to communicate effectively with Nicodemus, Zaccheus, and the woman at the well in John 4 because he understood their religious and cultural backgrounds, so love demands our patience and involvement to do the same. What kind of Mormon are you dealing with? Remember there are at least three levels of Mormon: temple-worthy Mormons, moderate Mormons, and nominal Mormons.

Temple-worthy Mormons. Temple-worthy Mormons reflect the highest level of commitment. They will tithe, regularly attend the sacrament meetings of the church, and send their children on Mormon missions. To lead these people to Christ means a long-term involvement. You will have to become their friend and win their trust.

As well, you will need to understand Mormonism. LDS will challenge your faith so that you will need to answer why you believe God is uncaused and is uniquely God; you will have to explain why the Jesus of the Bible is different from the Jesus of Mormonism and why faith in him is the sole means to salvation. You will need to raise questions about Mormonism and explain why you cannot trust the *Book of Mormon,* or believe that Joseph Smith was a true prophet of God, or accept the Mormon gospel as true.

Remember, too, that Mormonism is not just a nonbiblical cult—it is also a culture. Most active Mormons have all of their family, social, and business connections with other Mormons. They spend three to four days a week involved in the church. Often they are employed by or employ other Mormons. For them to alter or weaken these ties by renouncing the theology of Mormonism and leaving the Mormon Church requires a great sacrifice. Your friendship and personal encouragement of them will be extremely vital in their decision to follow Christ.

Moderate or minimalist Mormons. Many Mormons love their church, its history, and the Mormon culture but do not believe the totality of Mormonism per se. These can be classified as moderate or minimalist Mormons. They support only a small part of the church's doctrinal line, or a minimum level of belief. They might often be referred to as liberal Mormons. They will be more open to discuss doctrines with you but are often skeptical about the truthfulness of the Bible and the claims of biblical Christianity.

Nominal or "Jack" Mormons. Since the time of Brigham Young, inactive Mormons have been called "Jack" Mormons. Many of these people still are committed cultural Mormons. They may believe the *Book of Mormon* but are no longer active in the church. Relationship-building with them will be important.

Others among them have become disgruntled or skeptical about the claims of Mormonism. They may have completely turned their backs on organized religion. For them to experience genuine and unconditional Christian love will be revolutionary and life-changing. Be prayerful and patient with them. Seek an opportunity to share God's plan of salvation. Be ready to respond to their questions about the Bible and the Christian faith. They may ask any of these four questions:

1. How can I know the Bible is true?
2. How do I know that Jesus is who he says he is?
3. How can I be saved by faith in Christ alone? Don't I need to do something to merit salvation?
4. Why are there hypocrites in the church?

You should be ready to answer these questions with gentleness and respect.

SHARING THE GOSPEL

Fifty thousand young Mormon proselytizers cover the globe. They have learned a set approach to presenting Mormonism. They stay in pairs at all times so that neither one will waver or compromise his faith. They have been instructed not to argue or to read or view "anti-Mormon" or non-Mormon material. How should you respond when Mormon missionaries come to your door?

If you are not yet confident in evangelizing Mormons, simply tell them you are not interested, share a two-minute testimony of how Jesus has changed your life, and, after finishing, politely excuse yourself, close the door, and pray for them as they walk away.

If you are confident in sharing the gospel with Mormons but don't have much time, make an agreement with them. Let them take ten uninterrupted minutes to tell you why you should become a Mormon in exchange for ten minutes of your telling them—uninterrupted—why they should trust the Jesus of the Bible as their Savior. Give them a gospel tract—if they'll take it—and then before they leave, pray for them to be saved.

If you are confident in sharing the gospel with Mormons and have more time, invite them to join you in a Bible study on the Bible's plan of salvation (see the following section on sharing the plan of salvation); and, if you wish, go from there to show them how the *Book of Mormon* agrees with the Bible about salvation. Befriend the missionaries and invite them to an evangelistic service at your church. Remember, "faith comes by hearing the word of God" (Rom. 10:17). Tell your pastor they are coming, and organize a prayer group for them. Mormon missionaries can be extremely lonely, and your sincere and personal interest in them can open a door for the gospel.

The following five points may help you in sharing your faith and the truth of Jesus Christ with Mormon missionaries and any other Mormon you know.

Focus on the Central Doctrines of the Faith

Keep the main thing the main thing. In seeking to win Mormons to Christ, don't get involved in discussing temple undergarments or secret handshakes or the hidden and sordid secrets of the life of Joseph Smith. Sharing the gospel must take priority over all other elements of your discussion. If your neighbor's house is on fire, it might be nice to mow his grass to help him feel better, but it would also be a tragic misplacement of priorities. Your first priority would be to get him out of the house and to call the fire department. Keep first things first!

Apply Pascal's Wager in the Mormon Context

Blaise Pascal was a seventeenth-century Christian philosopher who developed a particular argument for use with unbelievers. Pascal confronted unbelievers with this argument: If Christianity is true, then an unbeliever has everything to lose—both peace and contentment in this life, as well as the reality of heaven after death. If Christianity, on the other hand, is not true, he argued, the Christian believer has lost nothing. Instead, the Christian still has peace and contentment in this life while the unbeliever lives with forlornness and fear about the future and life beyond death. Pascal said that this presented the prospect of a divine wager. The odds, if you will, even if they are even, leave the believer with a far brighter prospect. The unbeliever has nothing to gain if God doesn't exist, but he has everything to lose if God does exist and the unbeliever remains in an unrepentant state.

The same argument or wager may be used with the Mormon. If Mormonism is true, the non-Mormon has nothing to lose. When non-Mormons die, if they have been good persons, they will inherit the terrestrial kingdom. And, in fact, during the Mormon millennium, they will be baptized by proxy and have the opportunity to enter paradise. After the final judgment, they may be exalted to the celestial kingdom. The only danger for anyone, then, to be condemned to an eternity in outer darkness, would be to join the LDS Church. For once a member of the church has experienced the burning in the bosom and then turned against Mormonism, that member becomes an apostate. The apostate is headed, according to Mormonism, for an eternity in perdition or "outer darkness." What should be, in the minds of Mormons, the most spiritually secure place in the world—membership in the LDS Church—actually becomes the most dangerous.

For the Mormon, however, to reject the gospel of the Bible is to reject God's full and complete gospel of grace. While Jesus died on the cross for the sins of the world, the Jesus they believe in is not truly God from all eternity. Hence, the Jesus of Mormonism is incapable of full atonement. In fact, Mormonism itself agrees tacitly with that opinion. Why? Because according to LDS theology, sinful and debauched persons must pay for their own sins through suffering in spirit prison throughout the Mormon millennium. God and righteous people merit or earn their own way to the terrestrial kingdom. Their salvation comes by having lived a good life. Additionally, it is baptism and involvement in the LDS Church that gains entrance into the celestial kingdom.

The Bible does not present, or offer, a second chance after death for salvation. In fact, faith, the essential ingredient to please God and without which we cannot be saved (Eph. 2:8–9; Heb. 11:6), is not possible in the life to come. After a person dies, he or she faces God in judgment (Heb. 9:27). Faith is then replaced by seeing and knowing.

Mormons have eternity to lose. The eternal wager is against them.

Share the Plan of Salvation

Many Mormons have not heard, nor do they understand, the gospel of the Bible. To share it with them is vitally important. But we must remember that when the biblical plan is shared, there are certain truths that have particular relevance for the committed Mormon. It is important that we share the gospel by emphasizing certain points so that our Mormon friends do not miss the essence of the good news.

First, clarify for the Latter-day Saint the reality of sin and the utter seriousness of the sinfulness of the human race. Remember that Mormonism teaches a truncated and flawed view of sin. Nothing could be more dangerous. Imagine if you were seriously ill and did not know it. You would not seek help or proper medical attention. That is why self-righteousness is more dangerous than unrighteousness, and that is why Mormonism is so deceptive for the Mormon himself. Mormons must know that they have sinned and fallen short of the glory of God. They must know that the natural and unredeemed state of humankind is alienation from God (John 3:17–21; Jer. 17:9; and Rom. 3:10, 23; 5:6–12).

Second, show the Mormon that in God's love, Christ died for all the sins of the world—not just for Adam's original sin. This fact is clearly declared in the Bible (John 1:29; 1 John 2:1–2). If indeed this is God's truth, then no one—not even Mormons—can earn or merit their way into forgiveness with God. If Christ is the sole and complete sacrifice for sin, our works to achieve what he already has are vain and useless (Eph. 2:8–9; Titus 3:5–6).

Third, show the Mormon that salvation is accessed by faith and belief. Salvation is not a universal condition that is imposed upon people. It is conditioned by our willingness to receive and accept it. Just as any gift must be believed by its recipient to be authentic, and just as it is accepted, opened, and taken to be one's own, so God's salvation needs to be believed and received (John 1:12; John 3:16–18; Eph. 2:8–9; Rev. 3:20). Salvation is never referred to in the Bible as universal. That's because we must accept Jesus Christ as Lord and Savior to experience it!

Fourth, show the Mormon that without the Christ of the Bible, he or she is separated from God's forgiveness now and will be separated from him in eternity (John 3:36; 1 John 5:12; Luke 13:3). To believe or hope otherwise is to contradict the Bible itself.

Fifth, using the Bible, show Mormons that they may be saved now by believing in Christ, trusting him for their salvation, and asking him to be the Lord and Master of their lives. By trusting Jesus, they immediately receive the full pardon of all their sins. They also experience complete and total assurance. If they should die immediately, they will go to be with God in heaven—not a third-rate, tourist-class level of existence, but into the presence of the Father, Jesus, and the Holy Spirit (1 John 5:13; Luke 16:19–22; John 3:36; John 14:1–6).

Sixth, show Mormons that they must confess Jesus Christ as Lord and Savior. The Scripture is clear, "with the mouth confession is made unto salvation" (Rom. 10:10). Just as a couple moving through their marriage ceremony must confess their commitment to each other, God demands no less of those who desire to know Jesus as Lord and Savior. They are then directed by him to follow him in believer's baptism and in discipleship, not to be saved, but as evidence that they are saved (Rom. 10:8–13; Matt. 10:32–33; 28:18–20; Acts 8:36–38).

Pray with your Mormon friend a sinner's prayer that reflects the essential elements of the gospel:

> Lord Jesus, I believe that you are eternal God and that you died on the cross for all of my sins. I believe that God the Father raised you from the dead. Please forgive me of all my sins. I trust you alone for my salvation. I turn from my sins and self-reliance to you as my only hope for full salvation. Come now into my heart and life. I invite the Holy Spirit to fill me and lead me. Please take me to heaven when I die— into the very presence of the heavenly Father. Thank you for hearing my prayer, saving me, and giving me eternal life. In Jesus' name, amen.

Seventh, share with Mormons who prayed the above prayer that when they trusted Christ, the Holy Spirit came into their heart and life. They have the full assurance of eternal life because they have Jesus and have believed in him (1 John 5:13).

Don't Spend Time Arguing Issues

Some Mormons do not believe or accept all Mormon doctrines or beliefs. If you are witnessing to a person who does not hold to a particular Mormon position, like the idea that God was once a man or that Jesus is his literal offspring, do not spend time arguing those particular issues. Just clearly show him that the Bible does not teach these ideas and move on to encourage him to accept the Jesus of the Bible and his total payment for sin as the basis of salvation. Make certain they do understand and embrace the biblical view of God, Jesus, and the plan of salvation.

Use the *Book of Mormon*

It may be useful to show the Mormon that the *Book of Mormon* teaches the basic and essential truths about salvation as found in the Bible.

Ask the Mormon to turn in the *Book of Mormon* to Mosiah 27. In that chapter a Nephite prophet named Alma describes his experience with God. He quotes the Lord telling him: "Marvel not that all mankind, yea, men and women, all nations, kindreds, tongues and people, must be born again; yea, born of God, changed from their carnal and fallen state, to a state of righteousness, being redeemed of God, becoming his sons and daughters; and thus they became new creatures; and unless they do this, they can in nowise inherit the kingdom of God" (Mosiah 27:25–26).

Then turn back to Mosiah 3 where an angel addresses King Benjamin and tells of the coming of Christ. The angel clearly states that Jesus Christ will be God himself incarnate (Mosiah 3:5,8) who shall heal the sick, and cast out demons, and do miracles (3:5b-6). He will suffer temptation, die as an atonement for man's sin, and be raised from the dead after three days (3:7, 9, 11). He then shall stand as man's righteous judge (3:10). "But wo, wo unto him who knoweth that he rebelleth against God! For salvation cometh to none such except it be through repentance and faith in the Lord Jesus Christ" (Mosiah 3:12). Later the angel reiterates his statement that salvation is only through Christ. "And moreover, I say unto you, that there shall be no other name given nor any other way nor means whereby salvation can come unto the children of men, only in and through the name of Christ, the Lord Omnipotent" (Mosiah 3:17).

Note that the above verses indicate that what is needed for salvation is repentance from sin and faith in Jesus Christ as Lord and Savior. Baptism, church membership, temple work, or other LDS doctrines are not mentioned. Though we certainly cannot rely on the *Book of Mormon* as an authoritative text, we can show the Mormon that when it was published (1830), Joseph Smith still had a fairly orthodox understanding of salvation. Later he altered it to fit his evolving system. Point out to the Mormon that the biblical way of salvation still stands, Joseph Smith notwithstanding, and that salvation still requires a new birth in Christ.

SALVATION IS NEAR

Mormons can be and are won to Christ. But they can only be won if Christians are equipped to tell them the gospel, are encouraged supernaturally by the Holy Spirit to do so, and are willing to be obedient to share the good news with them. You may be the person God will use to witness effectively to them. Be prayerful and consistent in your witness for Christ.

Paul Read's book *Alive!* tells the story of a rugby team from Uruguay that went down in the Andes Mountains in a plane crash. The survivors were east of the highest peaks of the great mountain range. For weeks and months they struggled to go west and make contact with civilization. If they had gone east, they would have located an emergency shelter with food not too far away. Rescue would have come sooner and lives would have been saved.

Mormons believe they must scale the mountain of perfection and total obedience to Mormonism to know God and the fullness of this salvation. But Jesus paid the full price for their sin. They can trust him and be saved fully. Works, then, would come out of gratitude and not from fear. But before they can believe, they must hear that salvation is near if they turn to the true Christ: "'The word is near you; it is in your mouth and in your heart' . . . if you confess with your mouth 'Jesus is Lord,' and believe in your heart that God raised him from the dead, you will be saved" (Rom. 10:8–9 NIV).

Keep lovingly pointing Mormons to the Christ of the Bible's gospel. In him they will finally find the salvation that eludes them and yet is so near.

NOTES

Chapter 1

1. Joseph Smith Jr., *Book of Mormon* (Salt Lake City: Church of Jesus Christ of Latter-day Saints, 1981), 529.
2. *Uniform System for Teaching the Gospel,* Discussion 1: "The Plan of Our Heavenly Father" (Salt Lake City: Corporation of the President of the Church of Jesus Christ of Latter-Day Saints, 1986), 1-1.
3. Ibid., Discussion 2: "The Gospel of Jesus Christ," 2-1.
4. Ibid., Discussion 3: "The Restoration," 3-1.
5. Ibid., Discussion 4: "Eternal Progression," 4-1.
6. Ibid., Discussion 5: "Living a Christ Like Life," 5-1.
7. Ibid., Discussion 6: "Membership in the Kingdom," 6-1.

Chapter 2

1. *Time* magazine, 4 August 1997, 53.
2. Ibid., 52
3. For more information see *Dialogue,* vol. 29, no. 1, spring 1996.
4. Stephen Robinson, taped interview, 26 June 1997.
5. Joseph Smith—History 1:19, *Pearl of Great Price* (Salt Lake City: Church of Jesus Christ of Latter-day Saints, 1981).
6. "Christian but different," *USA Today,* 22 October 1997, 2-D.
7. I am thankful to Bill Gordon of the Interfaith Witness Evangelism Team of the North American Mission Board, SBC for his detailed analysis of *The Divine Center.*
8. Stephen Covey, *Divine Center* (Salt Lake City: Bookcraft, 1982), 17.
9. Ibid., 67–68.
10. Ibid., 68.
11. Ibid., 208–9.
12. Ibid., 240.
13. Darl Anderson, *Soft Answers to Hard Questions,* 31.

14. Ibid., 31.
15. AP story, "Mormons urge use of formal name," 5 October 1997.
16. *Deseret News* (Salt Lake City), 15 November 1997.

Chapter 3

1. Fawn M. Brodie, *No Man Knows My History: The Life of Joseph Smith, the Mormon Prophet* (New York: Alfred A. Knopf, 1971), 6–33. See also Jerald and Sandra Tanner, *Mormonism—Shadow or Reality?* (Salt Lake City: Utah Lighthouse Ministry, 1987) 32–49.
2. Joseph Smith—History 1:5–19, *Pearl of Great Price* (Salt Lake City: Church of Jesus Christ of Latter-day Saints, 1981).
3. Ibid., 1:33–35.
4. *Doctrines and Covenants* (Kirtland, Ohio: F.G. Williams & Co., 1835), 52–58. See also Tanner, *Mormonism—Shadow or Reality?* 143–62.
5. Tanner, *Mormonism—Shadow or Reality?* 151–52.
6. Lev. 19:26; 20:6, 27; Deut. 18:10; Isa. 19:3.
7. Tanner, *Mormonism—Shadow or Reality?* 32–49.
8. Linda King Newell and Valeen Tippetts Avery, *Mormon Enigma: Emma Hale Smith, Prophet's Wife, "Elect Lady," Polygamy's Foe, 1804–1879* (Garden City, N.Y.: Doubleday, 1984).
9. Ibid., 41.
10. David Whitmer, *An Address to All Believers in Christ* (Richmond, Mo.: David Whitmer, 1887), 12.
11. Michael Marquardt and Wesley P. Walters, *Inventing Mormonism: Tradition and the Historical Record* (Salt Lake City: Smith Research Associates, 1994), 55, 61, n. 49.
12. Joseph Smith, *Doctrine and Covenants* (Salt Lake City: Church of Jesus Christ of Latter-day Saints, 1981), 22:1–4.
13. Ibid., 13; 27:8; 84:18; Joseph Smith—History, 1:68–70, *Pearl of Great Price*.
14. *Doctrine and Covenants*, 115:4.
15. Ibid., 35, 37, 41, 42, 45, 73, 74, 76, 77, 86, 91, 93, 94, 104, 124.
16. Richard S. Van Wagoner, *Sidney Rigdon: A Portrait of Religious Excess* (Salt Lake City: Signature Books, 1994), 19–36.
17. *Doctrine and Covenants*, 37:3; 38:31–32.
18. Ibid., 57:1–3.
19. Ibid., 84:3–5.
20. *Church History in the Fulness of Times* (Salt Lake City: Church of Jesus Christ of Latter-day Saints, 1989), 131.
21. *Doctrine and Covenants*, 103.
22. *Church History in the Fulness of Times*, 141–51.
23. Joseph Smith, *History of the Church*, vol. 2 (Salt Lake City: Deseret Book Co., 1978), 182.
24. Whitmer, *An Address*, 56–62.

25. *Doctrines and Covenants* (Kirtland, Ohio: F.G. Williams & Co., 1835), 251.
26. Todd Compton, "A Trajectory of Plurality: An Overview of Joseph Smith's Thirty-three Plural Wives," *Dialogue: A Journal of Mormon Thought,* 29, no. 2, summer 1996, 2.
27. Tanner, *Mormonism—Shadow or Reality?* 203; see also Brodie, *No Man Knows,* 181–85; Newell and Avery, *Mormon Enigma,* 66.
28. Tanner, *Mormonism—Shadow or Reality?* 245–48.
29. Smith, *History of the Church,* vol. 2:236.
30. *Pearl of Great Price,* preface to Book of Abraham.
31. *Dialogue: A Journal of Mormon Thought,* summer 1968, 68, 98; and autumn 1968, 119–20, 133.
32. Charles M. Larson, *By His Own Hand Upon Papyrus: A New Look At The Joseph Smith Papyri* (Grand Rapids, Mich.: Institute for Religious Studies, 1992), 61–111.
33. *Doctrine and Covenants,* 132:19, 20, 52, 61, 62.
34. Van Wagoner, *Sidney Rigdon,* 184.
35. Ibid., 218; Newell and Avery, *Mormon Enigma,* 72.
36. Brodie, *No Man Knows,* 234–35.
37. Ibid., 237–55.
38. *Pearl of Great Price,* Book of Abraham, 4:1.
39. *Doctrine and Covenants,* 132:52, 61, 62, 64.
40. George D. Smith, "Nauvoo Roots of Mormon Polygamy, 1841–46: A Preliminary Demographic Report," *Dialogue: A Journal of Mormon Thought,* 27, no.1, 15.
41. Brodie, *No Man Knows,* 356.
42. Smith, *History of the Church,* vol. 6: 303–5.
43. Ibid., vol. 6: 473–74.
44. Ibid., vol. 6: 607–621; vol. 7: 102–105.
45. Tanner, *Mormonism—Shadow or Reality?* 537–41.

Chapter 4
1. Bruce R. McConkie, *Mormon Doctrine* (Salt Lake City: Bookcraft, 1979), 576–77.
2. B. H. Roberts, Manual, 1901–2, pt. 1, p. 17, *Defense of the Faith and the Saints,* vol. 2, p. 273, as quoted in *LDS Collector's Library '97,* CD-ROM.
3. B. H. Roberts, *New Witnesses for God,* vol. 1, p. 461, in *LDS Collector's Library '97,* CD-ROM.
4. Joseph Fielding Smith, *Teachings of the Prophet Joseph Smith* (Salt Lake City: Deseret Book Co., 1977), 345–46.
5. Sterling M. McMurrin, *The Theological Foundations of the Mormon Religion* (Salt Lake City: University of Utah Press, 1965), 36.
6. *Doctrine and Covenants,* 130:22.
7. Eldred G. Smith, *BYU Speeches,* 10 March 1964, p. 6, in *LDS Collector's Library '97,* CD-ROM.

8. *Doctrine and Covenants*, 130:3.
9. Joseph Fielding Smith, *Teachings*, 370–74.
10. Church of Jesus Christ of Latter-day Saints, *Search These Command-ments: Melchizedek Priesthood Personal Study Guide* (Salt Lake City: Church of Jesus Christ of Latter-day Saints, 1984), 153.
11. *Encyclopedia of Mormonism*, vol. 4 (New York: Macmillan, 1992), 1670.
12. *Ensign* magazine, November 1991, 97–100.
13. LDS Conference Report, April 1949, 27, in *LDS Collector's Library '97*, CD-ROM.
14. B. H. Roberts, *The Mormon Doctrine of Deity*, 255, in *LDS Collector's Library '97*, CD-ROM.
15. *Doctrine and Covenants*, 132:19.
16. Joseph Fielding Smith, *Teachings*, 346–48.
17. Ibid., 350.
18. *Encyclopedia of Mormonism*, vol. 1 (New York: Macmillan, 1992), 397.
19. *Encyclopedia of Mormonism*, vol. 2 (New York: Macmillan, 1992), 548.
20. Scott H. Faulring, ed., *An American Prophet's Record: The Diaries and Journals of Joseph Smith* (Salt Lake City: Signature Books, 1989), 5, 51, 59.
21. Joseph Fielding Smith, *Teachings*, 349.
22. "The Empire of the Mormons," *Time*, 4 August 1997, 56.
23. Church of Jesus Christ of Latter-day Saints, *Achieving a Celestial Mar-riage* (Salt Lake City: Church of Jesus Christ of Latter-day Saints, 1992), 132.

Chapter 5

1. Church of Jesus Christ of Latter-day Saints, *Gospel Principles* (Salt Lake City: Church of Jesus Christ of Latter-day Saints, 1992), 11–13.
2. Joseph Smith Jr., *Doctrine and Covenants* (Salt Lake City: Church of Jesus Christ of Latter-day Saints, 1982), 93:21, 22; 181.
3. *Gospel Principles*, 18–19.
4. Smith, *Doctrine and Covenants*, 93:21; 181.
5. *Gospel Principles*, 377.
6. Smith, *Doctrine and Covenants*, 130:22; 285.
7. *Gospel Principles*, 105–6.
8. Spencer W. Kimball, (speech delivered at "Paris France Area Confer-ence, August 1976), quoted in Rulon T. Burton, *We Believe: Doctrines and Principles of the Church of Jesus Christ of Latter-day Saints* (Salt Lake City: Tabernacle Books, 1994), 30.
9. Bruce McConkie, *A New Witness for the Articles of Faith* (Salt Lake City: Deseret Book Co., 1985), 67.
10. Stephen E. Robinson, interview in the video, *The Mormon Puzzle* (Alpharetta, Ga.: North American Mission Board, SBC, 1997).
11. Joseph Fielding Smith, *Doctrines of Salvation*, 1:18, quoted in Burton, *We Believe*, 329.

12. *Gospel Principles,* 73; *Doctrine and Covenants,* 19:18–19, 32.
13. Joseph Fielding Smith, *Doctrine and Covenants,* quoted in Burton, *We Believe,* 48–49.
14. Joseph Smith Jr., *Book of Mormon: Another Testament of Jesus Christ* (Salt Lake City: Church of Jesus Christ of Latter-day Saints, 1982), 3 Nephi; 4 Nephi.

Chapter 6
1. Joseph Smith, introduction to *Book of Mormon.*
2. *Doctrine and Covenants,* 1:17–18, 21–23.
3. Church of Jesus Christ of Latter-day Saints, *Doctrines of the Gospel Student Manual: Religion 231 and 232* (Salt Lake City: Church of Jesus Christ of Latter-day Saints, 1986), 60, quoted in Spencer W. Kimball, *The Teachings of Spencer W. Kimball,* 423.
4. *Gospel Principles,* 106.
5. Joseph Smith, "Religious History" 1:19, in *Pearl of Great Price.*
6. Ibid., 1:66–75.
7. *Doctrines of the Gospel,* 63.
8. Joseph Smith, "History" 1:69, in *Pearl of Great Price.*
9. See Romans 3:23; 6:23; John 3.
10. *Doctrines of the Gospel,* 13, quoted in Joseph Fielding Smith, *Church History and Modern Revelation,* 1:401. See also Book of Moses, chap. 3 and Abraham, chap. 3 in *Pearl of Great Price.*
11. Bruce R. McConkie, *Mormon Doctrine,* 2d ed. (Salt Lake City: Bookcraft, 1966), 589. See as a reference in the standard works *Book of Mormon,* Ether 3:16; and *Doctrine and Covenants,* 131:7–8.
12. *Doctrines of the Gospel,* 14, quoted in David O. McKay, *Home Memories of President David O. McKay,* 228–30.
13. Bruce McConkie, *A New Witness for the Articles of Faith,* 45.
14. *Doctrine and Covenants,* 27:11.
15. McConkie, *A New Witness,* 47.
16. *Doctrines of the Gospel,* 20, quoted in Joseph Fielding Smith, "Fall—Atonement—Resurrection—Sacrament" in *Charge to Religious Educators,* 124.
17. "Church News," *Deseret News,* 31 July 1965, 7.
18. A helpful outline of the Mormon gospel is contained in *Doctrines of the Gospel,* chap. 9, pp. 22–26.
19. Ibid., 22.
20. Ibid.
21. Ibid., see also *Doctrine and Covenants,* 29:46–50; 19:15–19 and *Book of Mormon,* Alma 7:12–13.
22. *Doctrine and Covenants,* 19:15–20; *Book of Mormon,* Mosiah 3:19 and 2 Neph. 9:21.
23. McConkie, *Mormon Doctrine,* 669.

24. *Doctrines of the Gospel*, 25–26. (See also chap. 4 in this book for an understanding of Mormon polytheism.)
25. See, for example, Matt. 25:31–32, 46; Rom. 2:5–11; 2 Thess. 2:7–10; Rev. 14:9–12.
26. *Gospel Principles*, 297.
27. *Doctrines of the Gospel*, 90; see also *Doctrine and Covenants*, 76:77–91; 88:99 and 45:54.
28. *Doctrines of the Gospel*, 90; *Doctrine and Covenants*, 76:99–101, 103.
29. Ibid.
30. *Gospel Principles*, 302; see also *Doctrine and Covenants*, 76.
31. *Gospel Principles*, 126.
32. James E. Talmage, *The Articles of Faith* (Salt Lake City: Deseret Press, 1976), 137.
33. *Gospel Principles*, 131.
34. Talmage, *Articles of Faith*, 167.
35. McConkie, *Mormon Doctrine*, 167.
36. Ibid., 227.
37. *Doctrine and Covenants*, 1312:1–4.
38. *Gospel Principles*, 195.
39. McConkie, *Mormon Doctrine*, 150.
40. McConkie, *Mormon Doctrine*, 796–98; *Doctrine and Covenants*, 64:23.
41. *Gospel Principles*, 155.
42. *Doctrines of the Gospel*, 85; see also *Doctrine and Covenants*, 128:1,5; 138:32–33.
43. This information was gleaned from the *International Genealogical Index of the LDS Church*.
44. *Doctrines of the Gospel*, 91; *Doctrine and Covenants*, 76:31–48.
45. *Doctrine and Covenants*, 29:36–39.
46. *Gospel Principles*, 77.

Chapter 7

1. Rulon T. Burton, *We Believe: Doctrines and Principles of the Church of Jesus Christ of Latter-day Saints* (Salt Lake City: Tabernacle Books, 1994), 73.
2. For further study of the textual reliability of the Bible see F. F. Bruce: *The Canon of Scripture* (InterVarsity Press, 1988) and *The New Testament Documents: Are They Reliable?* (InterVarsity Press, 1967).
3. Joseph Smith, "Religious History" 1:51, in *Pearl of Great Price*.
4. Jerald and Sandra Tanner, *3913 Changes in the Book of Mormon* (Salt Lake City: Utah Lighthouse Ministry).
5. Hal Hougey, *Archaeology and the Book of Mormon* (Concord, CA: Pacific Publishing, 1983), 12.
6. Department of Anthropology, Smithsonian Institution, "Statement Regarding the Book of Mormon" (Washington, D.C.: Smithsonian Institution, 1988).

7. Stephen L. Shields, *Latter-day Saints Beliefs: A Comparison Between the RLDS Church and the LDS Church* (Independence, Mo.: Herald Publishing House, 1986), 11.
8. Harry Ropp, *Is Mormonism Christian?* (Joplin, Mo.: College Press, 1995), 45.
9. B. H. Roberts, as reproduced in Hougey, *A Parallel: The Basis of the Book of Mormon* (Concord, Calif.: Pacific, 1963), 720, as quoted in Ropp, *Is Mormonism Christian?* 47.
10. Ropp, *Is Mormonism Christian?* 48.
11. Joseph Fielding Smith, *Teachings,* 194.
12. *Doctrine and Covenants,* 1:38.
13. Ibid., 89:5; 89:8; and 89:9 respectively.
14. Ibid., 124:36–40.
15. Ibid., 84:21–22.
16. Ibid., 107:1.
17. Ibid., 132:61.
18. Ibid.
19. Ropp, *Is Mormonism Christian?* 95.
20. Ibid., 90–108.

Chapter 8

1. Kent P. Jackson, "Avoiding Deception in the Last Days," in *Watch and Be Ready,* n. ed. (Salt Lake City: Deseret Book Co., 1994), 10–11.
2. *Doctrine and Covenants,* 45:27.
3. Ibid., 88:91.
4. Ibid., 88:90.
5. *Gospel Principles,* 267.
6. Ibid.
7. Ibid.
8. Ibid., 268; see also *Doctrine and Covenants,* 2.
9. Ibid.; see also 3 Nephi 21:23–25; and *Doctrine and Covenants,* 84:3–4.
10. See 3 Nephi 21:4; *Doctrine and Covenants* 101:76–80; and *Doctrine and Covenants,* 124:25–42 respectively.
11. *Gospel Doctrine,* 99, cited in John Taylor, *Journal of Discourses,* 10:147.
12. Robert J. Matthews, "The Role of the House of Israel in the Last Days," in *Watch and Be Ready,* 85, cited from Bruce McConkie, "The Patriarchal Order" August 8, 1967.
13. *Watch and Be Ready,* 86, quoting *Journal of Discourses,* 7:290.
14. *Doctrine and Covenants,* 116; *Manual of Doctrine,* 100.
15. *Light on Latter-day Saints,* 70–71 n. 151.
16. *Manual of Doctrine,* 101, cited from Bruce R. McConkie, "The Millennial Messiah," 578–9.
17. *Doctrine and Covenants,* 133:17–18.
18. Ibid., 45:48; see also *Manual of Doctrine,* 101.
19. *Doctrine and Covenants,* 45:44, 49–50.

NOTES

20. *Gospel Principles,* 277; *Doctrine and Covenants,* 101:24–25.
21. *Gospel Principles,* 279.
22. Ibid., 278–9, and *Doctrine and Covenants,* 76:50–70.
23. *Gospel Principles,* 278-79, and *Doctrine and Covenants,* 88:99; 76:71–80.
24. *Light on Latter-Day Saints,* 154–5.
25. *Gospel Principles,* 292; *Doctrine and Covenants,* 19:16–18.
26. *Gospel Principles,* 279; *Doctrine and Covenants,* 76:32–38, 81–112.
27. *Light on Latter-Day Saints,* 71 n. 157.
28. *Doctrine and Covenants,* 133:21; see also Robert L. Millet, "Life in the Millennium" in *Watch and Be Ready,* 182.
29. *Gospel Principles,* 282.
30. Ibid., 283, cited from Joseph Fielding Smith, *Teachings,* 268.
31. *Gospel Principles,* 282-3.
32. Ibid., 283.
33. Ibid.
34. *Watch and Be Ready,* 183; see also *Book of Mormon,* 2 Nephi 27:7–10; Ether 4:7, 15; 1 Nephi 5:17–19; Alma 37:4.
35. Ibid.
36. *Gospel Principles,* 285.
37. Ibid., 285–6.
38. Ibid., see also *Doctrine and Covenants,* 29:22–29; 88:17–20; 110–115.
39. *Gospel Principles,* 296.
40. Ibid.
41. Ibid., 298; see also *Doctrine and Covenants,* 76:28–35, 44–48.
42. *Gospel Principles,* 298.
43. *Gospel Principles,* 290.
44. *Doctrine and Covenants,* 138:30; see also *Gospel Principles,* 291.
45. *Gospel Principles,* 291. Segments of this quote are taken from Joseph Smith, "History of the Church" 4:209 and *Journal of Discourses,* 22:333–4.
46. *Gospel Principles,* 292.
47. *Gospel Principles,* 292–93.

Chapter 9
1. James E. Talmage, *The Vitality of Mormonism,* 27–28, in *LDS Collector's Library '97* CD-ROM.
2. *Doctrine and Covenants,* 84:17.
3. Ibid., 107:1–20.
4. Ibid., 107:17.
5. *Gospel Principles,* 90.
6. McConkie, *Mormon Doctrine,* 480.
7. Ibid., 606.
8. Joseph Fielding Smith, *Doctrines of Salvation,* vol. 3 (Salt Lake City: Bookcraft, 1956), 108–9.
9. Ibid., 108, 170.

10. McConkie, *Mormon Doctrine*, 242.
11. *Doctrine and Covenants*, 107:39–56.
12. Ibid., 107:25.
13. Henry H. Halley, *Halley's Bible Handbook* (Grand Rapids, Mich.: Zondervan, 1965), 134.
14. "Why I Joined the Mormon Church," 2, in *LDS Collector's Library '97*, CD-ROM.
15. Boyd K. Packer, *BYU Speeches*, March 23, 1965, 3, in *LDS Collector's Library '97*, CD-ROM.
16. *Encyclopedia of Mormonism*, 510.
17. McConkie, *Mormon Doctrine*, 69–71.
18. Ibid., 780–1.
19. Brigham Young, quoted in *Achieving a Celestial Marriage*, 203.
20. Jerald and Sandra Tanner, *Evolution of the Mormon Temple Ceremony, 1842–1990* (Salt Lake City: Utah Lighthouse Ministry, 1990).
21. Joseph Fielding Smith, *Teachings*, 356.

Chapter 10

1. *The Mormon Puzzle*, 18.
2. Boyd K. Packer, "The Candle of the Lord," *Ensign Magazine*, January 1983, 54–55.

GLOSSARY

Atonement—Salvation by Grace

LDS: Christ's death brought release from the grave and provided for universal resurrection. Salvation by grace is universal resurrection. Beyond this, man must earn his place in heaven. We are saved by grace only after *all* we can do (2 Nephi 25:23; *Mormon Doctrine*, 669–71).

Bible: Salvation is not universal but received by an individual's exercise of faith in the person and work of Christ alone—through grace, not works. Salvation delivers believers from their sinful nature, particular sins, and the ultimate consequences of sin—physical death and everlasting torment (Rom. 1:16; Heb. 9:28; Eph. 2:8–9).

Authority—Priesthood

LDS: They believe only LDS have authority to baptize, ordain, etc. LDS have a two-part system of priesthood—Melchizedek and Aaronic (*Doctrines of Salvation*, vol. 3, 80–81; *Doctrine and Covenants*, 107:1–21).

Bible: Christ brought an end to the Aaronic priesthood and is the *only* High Priest after the manner of Melchizedek (Heb. 5:9; 2 Tim. 2:2).

Baptism

LDS: Must be performed by the LDS priesthood (2 Nephi 9:23–24; *Doctrine and Covenants* 20:68–74; *Mormon Doctrine*, 69–72).

Bible: Emphasis is on the believer, not priesthood authority (Mark 16:15–16; Acts 2:37–41).

Born Again

LDS: By baptism into the LDS Church (*Mormon Doctrine*, 101).

Bible: We are spiritually dead until our spiritual rebirth by believing in the grace and work of Christ and asking him into our hearts (1 Pet. 1:23; 2 Cor. 5:17).

Eternal Life

LDS: Exaltation in the celestial kingdom; godhood and ability to bear children in heaven. Must have a temple recommendation and be sealed in a Mormon temple (*Doctrine and Covenants* 131:1–4; 132:19–25, 30, 55).

Bible: Not limited to certain ones in heaven. No mention of parenthood or temple marriage, but eternal life is given to *all* Christians (1 John 5:12–13).

The Fall

LDS: The Fall was a blessing. It brought mortality and physical death. God gave Adam conflicting commandments, and Adam made the best choice for humankind (*Doctrines of Salvation*, vol. 1, 111–15; *Gospel Principles*, 31–33; 2 Nephi 2:25; *Mormon Doctrine*, 268–69).

Bible: God tempts no one (James 1:13–14). Adam and Eve disobeyed a clear command of God, which ushered in misery and death for the rest of humanity. As a consequence, human beings became sinful creatures (Rom. 8:5–8; 1 Cor. 2:14).

Godhead

LDS: Father God is a resurrected man with a physical body; Christ is a separate resurrected man with a physical body; Holy Ghost is a separate man with a spiritual body. They are three totally separate gods (*Doctrine and Covenants* 130:22; *Teachings of the Prophet Joseph Smith*, 345–47, 370–73).

Bible: God is not a man (Num. 23:19). There is only one God (Isa. 43:10–11; 44:6; 45:21–22). God is an immaterial spirit and invisible (John 4:24; 1 Tim. 1:17). Father, Son, and Holy Spirit are three uncreated, eternal Persons existing in the same divine nature and sharing all the same divine attributes. The Son is the only Person in the godhead who has joined himself with a created human nature but without undergoing any changes in his divine nature.

Gospel

LDS: Doctrines and commandments of the Mormon Church. True gospel of Jesus Christ restored by Joseph Smith (*Mormon Doctrine*, 331, 334; *Doctrines of Salvation*, vol. 1, 156–59).

Bible: Message of Christ's death and resurrection as atonement for our sins (1 Cor. 15:1, 4; Gal. 1:8).

Heaven

LDS: Divided into three kingdoms: celestial, terrestrial, and telestial. There's a level of heaven for almost everyone (*Doctrine and Covenants* 76:39, 44, 50–112; and a misuse of 1 Cor. 15:40–41).

Bible: A place where those who have inherited eternal life through faith alone enjoy God's presence forever (Matt. 25:31–46).

Hell

LDS: Hell as an institution is eternal—inmates come and go as in jail, but they do not spend eternity there. Hell is temporary. One stays there only until one has paid one's debt to God (*Mormon Doctrine*, 349–51).

Bible: No mention of people leaving hell (Rev. 21:8; Matt. 13:24–43, 47–50; Luke 16:26).

Holy Ghost

LDS: A separate god from the Father and the Son. Different from the Holy Spirit. The Holy Ghost is a person; the Holy Spirit is an influence from God and is not a person (*Doctrines of Salvation*, vol. 1, 38–39, 49–52).

Bible: The same Greek word is used for *Holy Ghost* and *Holy Spirit* (1 Cor. 3:16; 6:19); they are one and the same Person, the Third Person of the blessed Trinity.

Immortality

LDS: Universal gift. The ability to live forever but not the same as eternal life. Immortals are unable to bear children (*Doctrine and Covenants* 14:7; 29:22–25, 42–43; *Mormon Doctrine*, 237, 376–77, 670).

Bible: Makes no distinction between immorality and eternal life (2 Tim. 1:10).

Kingdom of God

LDS: Means the same as celestial kingdom. Only those in the celestial kingdom are in God's presence. Those in the terrestrial or telestial kingdoms are not in the presence of the Father (*Doctrine and Covenants* 88:16–29; 131:1–4; 132:16–17).

Bible: All redeemed will be in God's presence (Rev. 21:1–3). All believers are part of God's kingdom (Matt. 13:41–43).

Pre-Existence

LDS: Everyone existed in a spirit world before receiving flesh-and-blood bodies (*Doctrine and Covenants* 93:29; Book of Abraham 3:21–22; *Teachings of the Prophet Joseph Smith*, 352–54).

Bible: Only Christ pre-existed, not human beings or any other creatures (John 8:58; Col. 1:17). We did not have a spiritual existence prior to earth (1 Cor. 15:46).

Redeemed

LDS: From mortal death only, not from sinful rebellion or spiritual death (*Doctrines of Salvation*, vol. 2, 9–19; *Gospel Principles*, 74–78; Articles of Faith, #2).

Bible: Christ redeems from more than mortal death; he redeems us from spiritual death too (Rom. 6:23; Eph. 2:1).

MORMONISM UNMASKED

Repentance

LDS: Concerned with individual acts, not concerned with a sinful nature (*Gospel Principles*, 39; *Doctrines of Salvation*, vol. 1, 133; vol. 2, 16–17).

Bible: Must admit and have a change of mind and heart concerning one's basic rebellion against God (Jer. 17:9; Luke 5:32).

Sin

LDS: Specific acts, not man's basic nature. One must know an act is wrong for it to be a sin (*Mormon Doctrine*, 550, 735–36).

Bible: We are in spiritual rebellion until our conversion (Eph. 2:3; Rom. 5:6). We do not just commit sins; we are basically sinful (Matt. 1:21).

Sons of God

LDS: We are all literal spirit children of God (*Mormon Doctrine*, 589–90).

Bible: We become a child of God at conversion (John 1:12).

True Church

LDS: Only the Mormon Church. The true church was taken from the earth until Joseph Smith restored it (*Doctrine and Covenants* 1:30; 115:3–4; *Mormon Doctrine*, 133, 136).

Bible: Not an organization; as born-again Christians, we are part of Christ's Body called the Church (1Cor. 12:12–14; Matt. 16:18; 18:19–20).

Virgin Birth

LDS: God, as a resurrected, physical man, is the literal father of Jesus, conceived in the same manner in which human beings are conceived on earth. Mormons believe that the account of the virgin conception in Matthew 1:18 is in error (*Mormon Doctrine*, 546–47, 742).

Bible: Says Mary was "with child of the Holy Ghost" (Matt. 1:18).

LDS References

Book of Mormon

Doctrine and Covenants

Mormon Doctrine by Bruce R. McConkie

Doctrines of Salvation by Joseph Fielding Smith

Teachings of the Prophet Joseph Smith by Joseph Fielding Smith

Gospel Principles (1995)